No One Knows…

A Family Hides Their Homelessness

Written by

Amy Kurtz & Glenn T. Schaefer

To Donnie,
Be a Blessing!

Acknowledgements

Similar to any big project, writing a book takes a village to complete it. I truly appreciate the support of my village throughout this journey. Last Christmas Eve, my dear friend Lori brought her friend Glenn over for soup and fellowship. Little did I know that Glenn would also become a friend of mine and eventually a co-author. I appreciate Glenn's sarcasm, energy, love for sports, and willingness to help. His encouragement has kept me afloat and his critiques helped keep me grounded.

Being a mom and teacher, my schedule is quite full, I am so thankful to my husband, Mike, for taking on more at home and supporting me. Our children are my biggest fans and cheerleaders, I am very proud of them and hope that they can be proud of me. I enjoyed sharing snippets of *No One Knows* throughout the writing process and receiving their approval.

I cannot accomplish anything without thanking the founder of the Amy Fan Club, my mama. She has always been by my side and supported me in every crazy adventure. I cannot wait for her to read what we wrote!

My close friends and friends, Stephanie, Becki and Elizabeth, who eagerly wait for me to finish and cheer me on continuously mean so very much to me. Thank you.

Lastly, I want to thank my students. My sixth grade math class was especially excited and offered up many suggestions for titles. I am thankful for their excitement and support. My seventh graders, a group of excellent writers, helped to remind me of how middle schoolers would act and think and helped me immensely as the characters were developed.

Illustration

Foreword

When the process of collaboration of this book began, I barely knew Amy Kurtz. She was a friend of a friend who offered a delicious bowl of soup with gracious hospitality to me at her home on an unseasonably warm Christmas Eve in Memphis. I was the new kid at the table, surrounded by teachers and pastors and kids. While I rarely lack in social skills, I wondered who knew about my past…my own trials and tribulations…my story of depression and homelessness.

No one likes to be judged and I was mortified that I wasn't "perfect" while sitting around that table of what seemed to be the chosen ones. Amy, however, made me feel comfortable and when she fired off her subtle but direct barbs of sarcastic comments about life, I knew sharing a book writing project with her needed to come to fruition. *"Oh, you're one of those People"* talked about my personal bout with depression and the fear of being judged. We wanted to expand upon that experience but also tell the story that very few ever hear about. The children who are the left out of society…the children of homeless parents and yes…it's much more prevalent that anyone would know.

Since Amy and I share a similar sense of warped humor and she is extremely adept at reaching out to the teenage set, I couldn't think of a better writing partner. Amy teaches seventh grade and walks the walk but more importantly, can talk the talk.

"No One Knows" deals with life situations of homelessness and depression, which corrupts the lives of so very many. We hope you enjoy this look in to a family who faces that scenario. As a relatively new author myself, I am honored to share this writing experience with Amy.

Glenn T. Schaefer

Chapter One: Normal

The aroma of blueberry pancakes and crispy bacon floats up to my room, quietly nudging me awake. I stretch out my arms and legs, my fingers and toes poking out the opposite ends of the black metal bunk bed, ready to jump off the top bunk and run down the cold wooden stairs for breakfast. My little brother, John, is stirring on the bottom bunk below me. He pops his head above the rail on my bed, "Good Mornin' Sunshine," he says, too cheerily, as he shoots foam Nerf darts in my face.

"Mama-a-a-a," I yell as I grab for the bright orange Nerf gun in John's hands. John hides the orange plastic weapon under his pillow as the sound of Mama's high heels, clacking on the stairs, approaches. He turns and smiles at Mama as she rounds the corner into our room.

"Boys, get ready for school, breakfast will be ready in five minutes. Tyler, stop pestering your little brother." Mama turns and exits. John smirks and I beam him in the head with one of his Nerf darts.

John grabs his wrinkled khaki school uniform pants from a pile on the floor and a clean red polo shirt with the yellow cross logo from the closet, slips them on with his socks from yesterday and clomps down the stairs leaving me alone in our room to finish getting ready. I carefully select my khakis and polo from my side of the closet and head to the hallway bathroom, only to realize I've been beaten by the queen of the bathroom, Sarah, my teenage sister.

There's three of us: Sarah, John and I, sharing one bathroom on the upper level of our two story brick home. Sarah 14, me 12, and John 10; each two years younger than the other- stair step kids, Mama calls us. As I stand in the hallway, arms crossed, leaning against the wall waiting for the bathroom, I gaze at a row of pictures- happy faces- from a moment in time when we were willing to stand next to each other for longer than a minute without pinching, prodding and wiggling. Mama says those moments were rare and very short and that for every nice smiley picture there were ten to twenty pictures with tears, the back side of John as he twirled around, and any one of us pinching the other one.

"Sarah," I pound on the bathroom door, "Come on, I need to shower before school," I yell over the music from her iPod which is blaring through the tiny purple Bluetooth speaker hanging on the wall next to the shower. After a painful five minutes of waiting, the queen finally emerges from the steamy bathroom- looking just as "wonderful" as always.

"Be patient, brat," Sarah bops me on the head as she struts down the hallway.

"About time you stopped looking at yourself, like that's gonna make a difference, snob." I mutter just loud enough so she could hear me, but not blaring to alert Mama's radar.

Finally, it's my turn, I take my quick shower- just long enough to not smell bad, but not too long so to miss breakfast and get in trouble. I take one last look in the mirror, smooth my strawberry blonde hair and join the family in the kitchen downstairs.

This morning Mama was whistling and humming a joyful tune, she must've looked at our report cards that came home yesterday- they displayed all A's and B's, even John's, which is a feat in itself. Mama loves to cook and sometimes she gets up real early and treats us to an amazing breakfast. Most days we just get ourselves bowls of cold generic corn flakes before we rush out the door for school. Today must be special. Mama loves to cook when she's happy! And I love it when I don't have to eat mushy corn flakes!

On this brisk winter morning, with the smell of Mama's cookin, we all rush to the table and savor the hotcakes she made for us. Daddy reads the morning paper and compliments Mama on her culinary efforts, John folds his bacon and eggs into his pancake and eats it with his hands like a giant taco with warm syrup dripping down his arm. Sarah lightly drizzles syrup on her sole pancake as she nibbles her breakfast. I, on the other hand, create Pancake Mountain with my golden short stack with slices of real butter melting in between each pancake, fluffy scrambled eggs and bacon and then smother it all in warm maple syrup like an edible volcano erupting with sweet nectar.

Mama finishes cooking and joins us at the table as we devour the last of the pancakes. We go around the table as we review the schedule for the day: Daddy has a required meeting at work. Last month's mandatory meeting resulted in his good friend Dwayne and nine others being laid off. We've been back at school for a week since Christmas break- the first week back is always hard to get back into routines, but this week will be easier and busier. Monday, we kids don't have anything after school. Tomorrow John will have basketball practice- he should practice a lot and Sarah will have cheerleading with her stuck-up friends after school. I will have guitar lessons too. Mama works today, but will be off in time to pick us all up from school. She always picks us up from school. Tomorrow, when we all have practices and lessons, Mama will work a little later and be off in time to retrieve us all from our extra-curricular activities. That extra hour of work will help Mama be able to pay for those activities we get to do.

After the breakfast dishes are cleared, we all split in different directions to find our shoes and quickly finish getting ready for school. I grab my three ring binder with my science homework from my meticulously organized desk while John hunts around our room for his math homework until he finds it peeking out from underneath his bed. John shoves his math book in his blue camouflage backpack as Sarah admires her own reflection for the thousandth time before heading for the door.

"Time to go," Daddy hollers as he throws on his black wool coat, kisses mama on the cheek and heads for the silver Lexus SUV that Daddy said he needed for work and Mama said we didn't need at all. We grab our lunches, Doritos, peanut butter sandwiches that we made ourselves and apples and carrots Mama forces us to take, and worn backpacks and follow him. She blows kisses out the window and away we go. Daddy drops us off at school, first Sarah at high school and then John and me.

John and I go to St. Paul Lutheran School. We ain't Lutheran, but Mama says learning about Jesus is good for us and it's a lot safer than our neighborhood school. Too many drugs floating around, even in a good neighborhood. Mama says privileged kids have too much money and don't know what to do with it. We ain't poor, but we ain't "privileged" either. We definitely ain't wasting our money on drugs that's for sure. They don't even let us buy cokes at the grocery store- just a waste of money and a dentist visit waitin' to happen. Mama and Daddy work hard for us and remind us of it frequently. Not having everything you want builds character- well, we certainly got a lot of character, that's for sure.

Anytime we want something at the store, we are reminded, "Money don't grow on trees." "Do you really NEED that?" The list could go on and on. Mama tells us that we are rich in blessings from above and Daddy works hard so that we have a roof over our heads and food in our stomachs.

Daddy works at a factory, supervising the assembly line. He has worked there for years and keeps expecting a promotion. His boss keeps telling him how great he is and how he just needs to wait a little longer for a higher position to become available. Each year he gets a tiny raise and keeps working hard, hoping for more money, but the big promotion never happens!

Every summer we go on a vacation with Daddy's annual bonus, it's a tiny bonus according to Daddy, but Mama has magical dollar stretching abilities and we get to do some awesome things with that minuscule amount of money. We've been to Disney

World, Gulf Shores, Alabama, St. Louis and Gatlinburg to name a few of our favorite vacation spots. Mama has a carefully scrapbooked vacation dream board that hangs above the desk in the kitchen- we each pin pictures and brochures of places we want to go. Mama pins coupons and deals for hotels, restaurants, mini-golf and any other "fun" looking thing she can think of that would save us a penny to help make the vacation possible. Then, in the spring we take a family vote, ultimately Mama and Daddy make the choice, but it's fun to dream!

As soon as we leave home in the morning Mama loads the dishwasher and wipes down the table, then she drives the ten minutes to work. Mama works at an office, answering phones while we are at school. All day long, Mama answers phones, "Thank you for calling K & H, this is Sandra, how can I help you?" She's always helping someone. When she's not at work, she's helping us at home or at school, or she's helping the neighbors with their kids.

At school, I glide into my 7th grade homeroom, hoping no one saw me walking with John as he tries to hook his lunch box to his belt. Seriously? Can that kid ever be normal?

"Hey, Julie," I croak out, trying to cover up the cracks in my voice. "Did you get your science homework done?" I stutter, trying to think of something intelligent to say that would impress a girl like Julie- a straight A, homework genius. Although, really I'm just a step behind her. Maybe that's why I like her so much- intelligence is so much more attractive than the ditziness that other girls my age seem to think is pretty.

Julie answers back, over her shoulder, "Of course, it was so easy. Do you need help, Tucker, I mean Tyler?"

"No, I got it, thanks." Although, a study date with her would be dreamy, until John came in picking his nose or belching the alphabet. Not a chance Julie would hang out with me, she's already busy talking to her clique of friends in the corner by the lockers. Chelsea jabbers on and on, practically shouting to her fan club circled around her, within 6 inches of her large mouth. She's going on about volleyball practice, playing for a club team, getting to go out of town and all the hours of practice she puts in- Julie smiles and nods at Chelsea's story, Shelby twirls her lengthy auburn hair around her ring finger and giggles when everyone else thinks something

Chelsea has said is funny. I do not understand girls, especially those girls- they seem to hang on every stupid word. Julie is better than that- Julie is sweet, smart and kind, but she's also popular and being popular means you have to hang with the other popular girls, even if they are ridiculous. Daddy says all girls are ridiculous, but the key to happiness is to pick the ridiculousness that makes you smile- Julie makes me smile!

"Hey Dude," Jack calls from over by our desks, where the boys are gathered. I saunter over to the guys and then realize that he was waving at Cooper, the cool kid behind me. I try to play off like I didn't just think he was talking to me and slink into the nearest desk, close enough to the guys to hear their conversation and feel like part of the group, but far enough away so they don't feel like I'm part of the group. It's hard being a nobody who wants to be a somebody or at least be noticed by a somebody. Some days I think I must be wearing an invisibility cloak- people just look right past me- like they can see through me and somehow miss that I'm right there in front of them begging to be acknowledged.

"Dude, did you study for the science test? Miss Berkham said it's gonna be easy, but I don't trust her. Her easy tests are always hard." Jack's words float out of his mouth, right under the fuzz on his lip that will one day be a mustache, the words dance towards my ears, but then poof- my thoughts take over and black out the conversation. My attention turns to basketball, Memphis Tigers, the Grizzlies and the Cleveland Cavaliers. The guys will be getting together this weekend to watch the Grizzlies play. Cooper's parents have season tickets and he gets to take a friend or two to the game. I wish he'd invite me. The smell of popcorn and the overwhelming noise of cheers filling the FedEx Forum would envelope me and carry me away to another world, a world filled with basketball fans. I wonder what it would be like to have the undivided attention of 18,819 people watching your every move, in awe of your incredible skills, chanting your name.

"Ty-ler, Ty-ler." My thoughts take me far, far away from my "nobody" reality to thinking of being noticed, being known, being….somebody.

"Tyler, hot lunch or home lunch, Tyler?" Mr. Malcolm calls me to attention. I wonder how long he's been saying my name. How long has his voice, his chanting been part of my dream?

"Home lunch, chocolate milk please." I respond perfunctorily as Mr. Malcolm takes lunch count and role before we officially begin our school day with prayers over the intercom and a short devotion in our homeroom. It's my routine to bring a lunch from home and get a delicious, cold chocolate milk to accompany my peanut butter and jelly sandwich. I'm not even sure why Mr. Malcolm insists on asking me every day, he should know what my response will be.

Beep, the sound of the school intercom breaks the classroom noise and calls for silence as Mr. Wheatley's voice floods the school, "Good Morning St. Paul, we begin this terrific Monday with the Lord's Prayer. Our Father, Who Art in Heaven….." The whole school prays in unison as we begin our day. Two hundred kids and teachers all praying the same words to the same God. To a stranger walking the halls it looks as if we are under a robotic trance, captured against our wills, however to God, it is sweet music of children confessing their desire to serve Him. And all the people say, "Amen."

The classroom chit chat resumes immediately after the intercom's final click. Mr. Malcolm attempts to get our attention, "Class, today you have a science test during first period......" I wonder if he knows no one is listening and just keeps talking to amuse himself. Mr. Malcolm is a nice guy, just seems clueless to keep yammering on like that when no one is listening.

"Uh, hum," Mr. Malcolm clears the imaginary phlegm from his throat to catch our attention as he grabs the little blue daily devotion book that he reads from each morning and begins to read, "January 13th, devotional thought for the day, Be Kind to Others." As the devotional thought is read, I look around the room at my classmates- their heads down "thinking" or more accurately trying to hide their iPhones underneath their desks while they text, tweet and post pictures from the weekend on Instagram. Every once in a while someone will raise their hand and answer, "Jesus," cause Jesus is always the right answer at a Lutheran School- sometimes it's right, other times Mr. Malcolm corrects them and moves on. I just sit up and listen to the devotion, I don't have an iPhone- Mama and Daddy say it's silly for kids to have fancy phones and I can always go to the school office if I need to call them. That's fine, I don't really want to be calling and texting people all the time- it's annoying to me, all of the idk's and lol's my classmates exchange throughout the day. Why can't we just converse with each other instead of sending abbreviated sentences through our devices? Oh wait, we are teenagers, and it's cool, that's why. The instant Mr. Malcolm finishes reading the devotion and prays with us, my classmates begin talking amongst themselves again, slipping their fancy phones into their school jacket pockets to hide them from Mr. Malcolm and the other faculty and staff at our school.

Ding-ing-ing, sounds the first bell, and everyone gets up from their desks, not halting their conversations, and moving in cliques to science class with Miss. Berkham. Miss Berkham stands stern in front of the class, holding the anticipated test in her right hand and taps the table with her pretty pink polished nails. She taps in a monotonous rhythm until the chatting dies to a low whisper.

How one person can demand attention just by lightly tapping and sternly staring at a herd of 7th graders amazes me!

The silence continues as Miss Berkham hands out the tests, reads us instructions as if we'd never taken a test before and everyone begins marking their best thought out answers, unless you are Steve- he just marks A-B-A-D-A-B-A, over and over again, saying it aloud, "abadaba, abadaba". Clicking and scratching of pens and pencils, flipping of test pages, tapping of feet, clearing of throats and an occasional whisper fill the room.

The day continues on: math, English, literature, Spanish, lunch, religion class, social studies, P.E. and art. Each class the same, students converse, the teacher instructs, homework is assigned and the bell rings for the next round. Art is my favorite- we get to do the coolest projects and Mrs. Frizzle, our art teacher, plays soothing music to help drown out chatter and bring out our creative sides. We get to express ourselves using paint, charcoal, pencils, paper and our own imagination.

At 3:15 each grade returns to their homeroom. We gather our homework, shove a mountain of books and notebooks in our backpacks and pray to end the day. As I heave my book-laden backpack over my shoulder, I'm surprised I don't fall over- my teachers love homework, I guess it makes them feel like they are teaching us well if we waddle to our cars groaning and gasping from the weight of our parcels. We line up at the classroom door, waiting to be released.

The school bell rings at 3:30 p.m. to dismiss us, classroom doors fling open and students pour out into the hallways. Excited noise fills the hallway as all of the grades are released at once. We file out to the sidewalk in front of the school and wait. All two hundred students line up, by class, outside the yellow brick school building waiting for their ride. Some kids watch excitedly as each car pulls in, hoping it's theirs and others are so involved in their conversation with their friends that they don't see that their ride has been waiting for them for ten minutes. Cooper's mama waves wildly out the window until Mr. Malcolm notices and shouts "Cooper, Cooper, your ride is here." Cooper puts his hand up to tell his mom, one minute, finishes his conversation with the guys and walks casually to his Mama in her White Suburban. I watch carefully for our ride and then grab John away from his goober friends as soon as the faded red minivan turns the corner into the parking lot.

When we get into Mama's half broken down seven seat minivan after school, Sarah is perched up front in the passenger seat, of course, since she's the queen and she gets picked up first. As the minivan slows to a stop, the back door jerks open- John and I heave our backpacks in, then I shove John in and climb in too, pushing the button in an attempt to close the van door. The door comes to a halt about halfway and I yank it closed. I sweep the crumbs off the seat where John sat yesterday while brother John just plops down not even noticing the gummies on the seat that will now be stuck to the rear of his pants. He'll probably eat them later for a snack. Sarah's got her earbuds in listening to "Radio Active" by Imagine Dragons and singing to herself- although we can hear her, so it's not so much to herself. I wish it was, because Sarah can sing about as well as a rock and she doesn't know it, even though we tell her all the time. I would be frightened if that voice came out of my own mouth.

"How was your day?" Mama asks to John and me, as she pulls away from St. Paul Lutheran School and onto the street.

"Great," John shouts, "Chase and I played four square at recess today with Brandon and Michael. Michael cried because I got him out, but we just kept playing anyway. Mama, can Chase spend the night Friday night? We wanna play Minecraft on the Xbox. You could pick us both up from school on Friday and we could play all night long!"

"We need to ask your daddy when he gets home." Mama replies. I really hope Daddy says no to the sleepover. The last time Chase spent the night I woke up to a web of toilet paper hanging from the ceiling in our room and stepped in a pudding cup on my way down from my bunk.

"Tyler? How about you? How was your day at school?"

"Just another day, Mama, nothing happened." I reply.

"How was your science test?"

"Easy." One word answers are a great way to stop the conversation when you don't have much to say. I don't tell Mama how I played basketball in the gym at recess and was subbed out after missing three shots in a row, so I just sat on the bleachers reading *Lightning Thief*, by Rick Riordan for the rest of the time. Mama doesn't want to hear about that.

"Sarah, how about you?" Mama inquires. Sarah doesn't say anything- good, I don't want to hear about her day with her snobby friends.

Mama turns the corner into our subdivision, Berry Hill. What a weird name for a neighborhood without berries and very few hills. We pass the rows of red brick houses, nicely groomed yards with kids playing in them. As our van pulls into the cove, our light blue garage door raises and Mama slowly glides into her spot on the right side of the two-car garage, leaving space for Daddy when he comes home from work at the end of the day.

Sarah exits the van first and walks straight upstairs to her bedroom, where she will proceed to hibernate until dinner time. That way she can talk on the phone to her boyfriend, Sean, avoid John and me and not do chores.

"What's for dinner, Mama? I'm starving," John whines as he climbs wildly out of the mini-van and dashes to the kitchen in search of a snack.

"Spaghetti, meatballs and garlic bread, dinner will be ready in an hour. You won't starve." Mama sighs, knowing that an hour is much too long for John to wait.

John grabs a pack of gummies and goes to the table to do his math homework for the day. I join him at the table, sitting on the opposite side, trying to give myself space to do my English work- we have to write a series of haiku poems. I start writing and tapping out the syllables. John smells like gummies- five syllables, He chews loudly to annoy- seven syllables, me and it works well- five syllables. I read my haiku out loud and John looks in my direction, smacking his lips even louder as if to prove my haiku even more poignant than it already was.

"Tyler, try writing something positive, you don't want your teacher to think we're just a bunch of animals." Mama says from the stove as she stirs spaghetti sauce in a medium black saucepan with her right hand and simultaneously uses her left hand to pour the whole wheat spaghetti noodles into a large pot of boiling water.

"Yes ma'am," I look down at my writing notebook and begin tapping again. Mama pours noodles- five syllables, Tyler writes Haiku poems- seven syllables, while his stomach growls- five syllables. I read it aloud to Mama, John flashes me a smile and sticks his tongue out at me.

"Very nice, Tyler," Mama says over her shoulder. "Now, put your homework away and help me set the table sweetie that should keep your growling stomach distracted." John immediately leaves the table and runs upstairs to our room like his pants are on fire- I think he's allergic to helping.

Mama smiles at me and I carefully place my spiral notebook and black pencil pouch into my backpack before grabbing the blue glass plates from the cupboard and begin setting the table. The smell of the spaghetti sauce distracts my mind and convinces me that I am hungrier than I thought I was. I enjoy the quiet of the kitchen while Mama cooks and I set the table. I pile John's homework up and toss it on the desk in the corner of the kitchen so there's room to eat at the table.

John, Sarah, Mama and I sit down at the table, in our designated spots, Daddy's spot is empty- Mama's eyes look troubled, like she is trying to hide her worries behind a smile. We eat our delicious homemade meatballs and spaghetti without a word about Daddy, just constant chit chat about our days and other nonsense. John entertains us with loud slurping noises as he sucks up his spaghetti and Sarah carefully chews each bite.

Some days, if I think real hard, I can still smell the pancakes from that morning and feel the kisses Mama blew to us. I can see mama's perfect makeup and her hair all done up. She always looked good when she went into work- hair and makeup done, pencil skirt and a button up shirt and those pretty shoes- mama used to have lots of pretty shoes. We could hear her click clack down the hallway in the morning.

That night, Daddy came home late, he missed dinner-time. He never misses dinner. His plate was still sitting on the table empty, with his glass of water, the ice has all melted- waiting for him. The rest of the plates had all been cleared and placed in the dishwasher by Sarah- it was her turn to clean up.

John and I race to the living room- the winner gets to rule the remote and choose what we watch. I use my elbows to block John from grabbing the remote from the couch, he whines, but I win, so it doesn't matter. I flip through until I find "The Flash," John likes it too, so he stops whining and drapes his body across the brown leather ottoman, laying on his stomach. I stretch my legs across his on the ottoman.

We can hear Mama and Sarah talking back and forth over the clank of the dishes as they clean up. The creek of the garage door dulls their conversation, as Mama glances towards the door to see

Daddy enter in, his face solemn- his eyes empty, he forces a smile and moves towards Mama.

Mama looks worried, but tilts her head as Daddy comes in and kisses her on the cheek. The smell of whiskey was hard on his breathe. Daddy takes a bottle out of the inside breast pocket of his coat and pours some whiskey into the glass he carried in his left hand and sits down in front of his plate.

Mama forces a smile on her face and spoons spaghetti onto Daddy's plate. She sits down across from him as he eats his cold dinner. Daddy is telling jokes and babbling about stupid stuff, just like one of us kids, his "Four Roses" glass never empty.

The smell of whiskey was a new scent for Daddy- before that day, he didn't usually drink- he would have a beer or two at the Fourth of July BBQ or share wine with Mama on her birthday. The whiskey smell wasn't the only unique thing about that night. When Daddy finishes his dinner, he joins us in the living room in front of the TV, but Mama shoos us to bed and kisses us each on the forehead as we tell her good night.

Mama must've wanted to talk to Daddy about something. After we all got settled in bed and our noise died down, we could hear them start to converse.

Laying in my bed I could hear their mumbles for hours. Finally, Daddy must've passed out and I could hear Mama's mumbles turn to tears. There weren't a lot of nights that Mama and Daddy would mumble, usually they would stay up late watching TV together on the couch, not tonight. I got up in the middle of the night for a snack and Daddy was laying half on the couch, half on the floor. He must've been too tired to go to bed with Mama. The Christmas tree was still lit- even though Christmas had passed, Mama liked to leave the decorations up for a little while- she loved the way the white lights lit up our dingy den. There lay Daddy, snoring peacefully with the lights of the Christmas tree illuminating the room. I snuck quietly to the kitchen, carefully opened the Oreo package, grabbed two cookies, and poured myself a small glass of milk for delicious dunking and returned to my bedroom, tip toeing quietly so Mama and Daddy wouldn't know I saw him.

I sat at my desk eating my late night snack, listening to John mumble and snort in his sleep. After sweeping the Oreo crumbs into the waste basket, I climb onto the top bunk, crawl sleepily into bed and count John's snorts until sleep takes over.

Chapter Two: Changes

Waking up, I stretched for a minute, craving the smell of pancakes, but it was nowhere to be found in our house. Our home was quiet, you could hear the tinkling of the spoon as John finished his cereal and the hum of Sarah's hair dryer from the upstairs bathroom. Daddy sat at the table with the newspaper, Mama marked big red circles all over one of the pages of the Careers section of the paper. Daddy had a blue marker in his right hand, crossing out the red circles, grumbling, "not enough money, too far to drive, those hours are out of the question." Mama is staring hard at me as I watch Daddy, my mouth wants to ask why he's grumpy, but Mama's eyes have frozen my lips shut.

Mama's face was pink and the puffy circles under eyes were filled with worries, sleepless worries. Mama's smile from yesterday, was faint this morning. She appeared less cheerful. Something changed, but no one was saying what. Daddy stayed home this morning, Mama dropped us off at school, without an utterance explaining why, just a faint smile and a farewell kiss to Daddy, and we went to school. Daddy's blue x's and mumblings and Mama's pink face and tired eyes suggest that something serious happened at Daddy's required meeting yesterday, but we know better than to ask about it.

A week goes by of Daddy staying home, red circles and blue x's on the employment section of the newspaper and Mama taking us to school.

One cool January Monday, on the way to school, Mama asks, "Do you remember Daddy's mandatory meeting about a week ago?"

"Yes ma'am," we nod hesitantly, afraid of the truth that would finally be told. We all knew Daddy lost his job, but we had become comfortable with hiding it. Scared that when the truth was finally said out loud it couldn't be taken back.

After a dramatic pause, Mama finally dropped the bomb of truth that we were hesitant to hear, "Daddy and ten other managers at his work have been laid off."

Sarah gasps, the drama queen that she is. John is playing a game on his DS and barely notices what Mama said. I stare out the window letting it all soak in. Laid off, those two words roll around in my 12 year old head- not valued, not noticed, pushed to the side. All of Daddy's hard work and the years he spent working his way up, in one day he was pushed off the cliff and instantly he was filing for unemployment. I imagine Donald Trump sternly bellowing, "You're fired," like on that T.V. show, "The Apprentice." I can see Daddy leaving the board room with his head down as Mr. Trump points his finger at him, hair never moving.

Mama continued, "Daddy's staying home right now, looking for a new job. He's been looking at the newspaper and searching for jobs on-line."

"Mama?" John began, "Is that why Daddy smells funny lately and talks goofy sometimes?" Daddy smelled like Whiskey most days, his "Four Roses" glass was by the sink every night.

Mama just nods and smiles. I don't think she wants to answer John, so she doesn't.

"John, Tyler, Sarah, we are going to need to make some changes for a little bit, save some money. Things are going to be tight, but I don't want to hear any complaints from y'all."

"Yes, ma'am," We agreed in unison. We aren't used to much, Mama had kept our lives pretty simple, but comfortable. A lot more comfortable than I ever realized, and a lot more luxurious than I ever appreciated.

We drop Sarah off at high school first, then Mama drops John and me off at St. Paul. John slides his DS into his backpack while Mama is looking the other way. "Have a good day, boys, love you."

"Love you Mama," John hollers as he hops out of the van and runs into school, eager to catch up with Chase and Michael.

"Bye, Mama," I reply as I grab my backpack and wave goodbye.

Walking into school Mama's words circle around in my head, "laid off…. things are gonna be tight….changes….no complaints."

"Hey man, what's up?" Cooper breaks my train of thoughts. "Whatcha doin this weekend? Some of us guys are gonna go catch a movie, wanna come?"

All I can think of is Mama saying, "changes." "Sorry, Cooper, I can't, we've got some stupid family thing goin on. I'll catch y'all next time."

"Alright man, sorry you're stuck with your family thing, we're gonna have a blast. I heard a group of girls are going too and we are gonna throw stuff at them during the movie!"

"Have fun!" Man, I wish I could go just to see the look on the girls' faces as they get bombarded with popcorn and paper airplanes. I'm pretty sure Mama's changes and cutting back don't include me going to a movie with my friends.

8:00 a.m. the morning bell rings. "Good Morning St. Paul Lutheran," Mr. Wheatley blares over the intercom. Mr. Malcolm takes his place at the front of the room, directing us to fold our hands, shut our mouths and bow our heads as we pray to begin our school day.

"Amen," the school says in unison.

"Lunch count" Mr. Malcolm begins calling out our names in alphabetical order.

The day goes on, just like any other day. No one knows my daddy just lost his job. No one knows our family is going to be making changes. I still don't really know what that means, but I suppose I will find out soon enough. Julie's dad lost his job last year, for about a month. I remember her being scared they would have to switch schools, but he found a new job and she got to stay.

I'm glad Julie stayed at St. Paul. I couldn't imagine seventh grade without Julie.

3:30 p.m. the seventh grade class is lined up at Mr. Malcolm's door- backpacks on- poised to go out into the world- well, at least the hallway. "Ring" the bell sounds and Mr. Malcolm opens the door to unleash us into the dismissal line in front of the school building. I find John and stand next to him as we wait for Mama's van to pull in.

"There's mom!" I point out the van to John as she pulls in.

"Bye Chase," John shouts as I pull him towards the van. We climb in. Mama smiles while Sarah is perched up front like usual, listening to her music.

"How was school?" Mama asks, as if nothing has changed.

"Good, Chase and I can sing our ABC's with our arm pit farts, wanna hear?" John pulls up his shirt and sticks his dirty hand in his arm pit.

"That's lovely John," Mama says, trying to ignore the weirdness of her youngest son. "John, put your shirt down, you should be learning at school, not making music with your underarms. Tyler? How about you? Did you learn any new songs you could play with your body parts?" Mama smiles at me through the reflection of the rear view mirror.

"Nope," I laugh, shoving John to get him to stop his "music."

"Mama? About what you said this morning about Daddy, I want you to know that we will help with whatever you want. Whatever changes we need to make, Mama, we will make them." I'm trying to sound grown up, so Mama won't worry so much about things having to be tight.

Chapter Three: Family Meeting

Things were tight, but Daddy never ran out of whiskey. Some days it was a big bottle and some days it was just the little one. Daddy wasn't real mean when he drank, he was either silly or sleepy, sometimes his words were mean or loud, but he never hit any of us. He seemed to drink to keep something in or protect his pride. It was like a cheap Band-Aid that couldn't heal the pain and it would fall off every morning, exposing the wound through his blood shot blue eyes.

Christmas was officially over, we had been back in school for a month. Daddy had taken all of the decorations down and put the boxes in the attic. The magic of Christmas was long gone. Our house was back to normal. Well, our new normal of Daddy being home. Nothing about it felt normal, I didn't want this to feel normal. I wanted Daddy to go back to work, Mama to be home more, I wanted pancakes in the morning for breakfast and to order pizza for dinner, but those luxury items had been cut.

The sing songy ring tone of the house phone interrupted the quietness of the house, followed by "Don't answer that, they just want money," Daddy bellowed from the couch.

Mama rushed to check the caller id, "MLG& W (Memphis Light, Gas and Water) they just want a payment again. Soon, they won't be able to bother us on the phone, 'cause we won't have one," Mama says as she shuffles through the pile of bills on the counter.

Mama sat back down at the kitchen table amongst a pile of papers with a pen, paper, calculator and her checkbook. Mama would hum the tune of "Amazing Grace," click the keys of the calculator, and jot down notes in her notebook. "Tyler, come empty the dish washer."

It's Saturday morning, time for our weekend chores as Daddy watches TV and Mama figures out our finances for the week. Mama was figurin' out a lot of things out these days, filling out a lot of paperwork to get us insurance, to have bills extended and any other grown up stuff you do when you have more month than money.

"John, Sarah, Tyler, come to the living room, it's time for a family meeting," Mama called through the house. John ran in from playing soccer in the backyard, Sarah strutted in, texting her friends and rolling her eyes at Mama for cutting into her "social" time and I put down, *Animal Farm* by George Orwell, a book I am reading for school.

I had been reading on the couch, so technically I got to the family meeting first, but Sarah pushed my feet off the couch, "Move over doofus," and John jumped over me to claim his spot on the ottoman. Daddy had been relaxing in his recliner, watching a basketball game on TV and Mama had just finished her calculating at the table.

"It's time to make a few of the cuts I told you kids about the other day." Mama began, "Sarah, you aren't going to be able to cheerlead anymore, the upcoming competitions are just too much for us right now."

"What? Why do you have to ruin my life? My friends are on that squad, I've worked so hard to get to go to Florida this spring, and now you and Daddy are gonna take it all away! I HATE YOU!" Sarah yelled as she stomped up the stairs. Mama wiped tears from her eyes and Daddy rubbed her shoulders, "It's okay, Sarah will come around, we are doing our best."

"Tyler," Daddy took over, "No more guitar lessons for this year, you can still play here at home, but we just can't afford the weekly lessons right now."

"Yes, sir." I reply, much less loudly than the drama queen because I know what it means to be supportive of each other and be a family. Besides, I can play guitar at home, look up songs on YouTube and play along. Drama Queen can't really cheer at home- at least I hope she can't.

"Mama, Daddy?" John asks, "What about me? What can I not do anymore?"

"Oh sweet Johnny," Mama replies, "Basketball season is just about over for you, and you can finish it, but you won't be able to play spring soccer or baseball this year, as soon as Daddy gets a new job, we will sign you up for something, ok, Johnny?" Mama put her arm around John, the baby.

"Ok Mama, I love you." John pecks Mama on the cheek and runs back outside to play.

He's such a kiss up.

At school, my teachers asked if I was okay as my homework wasn't always completed anymore and I didn't look as happy, I guess. I couldn't take guitar lessons anymore as our purse strings were tightened our extra-curricular activities were cinched out. Was something going on at home? How do I answer that? "Yes, my daddy's drinkin' instead of workin' and my mama's fake smile is expirin'." "Mac 'n Cheese and Hot Dogs is what's for dinner and a cup of Ramen Noodles for lunch." Of course, something is going on, or is it that nothing is going on at home? We don't talk about it, we aren't allowed to ask Daddy about his job hunt. "Just talk about happy things," Mama sang. So, most nights, I don't talk.

Sarah, John and I stay up late talkin. We don't have to talk about happy things if Daddy can't hear us. We talk about school, our teachers, the last time we had pancakes, and the other things we miss about when Daddy used to work. We talked about the empty whiskey bottles and how daddy talks too much when he drinks and keeps repeating himself. Sometimes he says funny things, and other nights he just rambles on and on. Daddy goes from yelling to laughing in 0.3 seconds and passes out, hanging half off the couch again like a pretzel man, in the middle of his favorite TV show.

Chapter Four: Rules

Mama took John and me to school each day on her way to work, but one cool February morning she parked our old minivan in the school parking lot and walked in with us. "I have a meeting with Mr. Wheatley," Mama said. Mr. Wheatley is St. Paul's principal, he seems very nice as he welcomes us to school each morning, but I've never had to go to his office and I've heard he's not so nice when you get in trouble.

"I didn't do it, I swear it was not me, Mama" I say very convincingly.

"Hush, Tyler, this meeting isn't about you, just get on into school." Mama replies trying to hurry us along to class. I open the door to school and hold it for Mama, like a gentleman should, and Mama and John walk into the front hallway.

John kisses Mama on the cheek, "Bye, Mama, I love you,"

"Suck-up," I whisper under my breath, lowering my head and hustling down the hall to my classroom.

Entering the 7th grade homeroom just before the bell sounds, I slide into my desk just in time to hear Mr. Malcolm call out for attendance and lunch count. "Tyler."

"Here, milk please." I reply respectfully and return to thinking about Mama's meeting with the principal, whatever it is that she has to meet with him about. Whatever it is, it wasn't me. I don't act up in school. I'm glad to be there- well, kind of glad. They make us read too much, but my friends are cool and my teachers aren't horrible. It was probably John, but he's the baby, so he don't get in much trouble at home, he just gets his way. That's what babies do, they get their way.

"Hey Tyler," Julie says, "Did you finish your math homework? I'm stuck on number sixteen."

"Yeah, I finished it. Number sixteen was tricky, let me show you how to do it." I say, trying to keep my voice steady as I get out my math homework to show Julie how to find the x in the algebraic equation.

"Thanks, Tyler," Julie sighs gratefully, closing her math book and filing her paper away in her portable file. She flips her ponytail and starts talking with the girls in our class about stuff I really couldn't care less about.

I open my sketch book and start drawing a tree as I wait for the bell for the first class to ring. Loudly- it blasts in the air. We all rise from our seats and file into the hallway as we head to Language Arts Class. An hour and a half of reading and writing, wow- that's a lot of time for words.

"Welcome, class!" Mrs. Hathaway begins, "Take out *Animal Farm*." She has a chart on the board of pigs, horses, ducks, and the political leaders and groups that they represent in the book. "Class, after reading a chapter in *Animal Farm*, I want you to work with a partner and create your own commandments or rules for your own society. What rules would be important to you? There are seven in the book, so you and your partner should create seven of your own rules to create a functioning society."

Cooper catches my eye from across the room, signaling that he wants to work with me. That's cool with me, Cooper is very creative and fun to work with and I'm smart, so lots of kids like to choose me to be their partner when it comes to schoolwork.

"Hey, dude, you write and I'll help you brainstorm rules." Cooper hops over the back of the chair next to me and leans on the table.

I grab a paper and pencil out of my binder and write, Cooper & Tyler's Commandments, at the top of the paper with big swirly letters. "Rule Number One: No whiskey."

"Yeah, that's good, I hate the smell of whiskey." Cooper agrees. Maybe his dad drinks it too, I don't ask and he doesn't ask me about it- I just write it down. "Rule Number Two: All women cook and clean."

"Cooper, Mrs. Hathaway might not like that rule, since she's a woman."

"Then she can't live in our society." Cooper retorts. "Write it down." My mama would smack him upside the head for that, she believes that both women and men should cook and clean, we should all share the responsibilities of the household. Pretty much, that means that us kids have to do chores so Mama and Daddy don't have to do everything themselves.

"Okay, Rule Number Three: All people should wear clothes." I say while laughing. "Well, in the book it says 'No animal shall wear clothes' but I don't want a society of naked people, so I think that is an important rule." Cooper busts out laughing, almost spitting his gum (that he's not supposed to have in school) across the room. Thankfully he catches his gum with his hand before it flies out of his mouth and sticks it under the table for a disgusting treat for the next person that sits in that spot.

"Gentlemen," Mrs. Hathaway strolls over to see what all of the commotion is about. The only bad thing about working with

Cooper is how loud he is, the teacher always comes over to see what he is up to. "What is all of this laughter about? What rules have you instituted for your society?" Mrs. Hathaway smiles as she moves close enough to gaze at our paper. "Hmmm, no whiskey, women are servants and you must wear clothes. Interesting choice gentlemen, continue on. I feel like you may not have a lot of women joining your society; you may go hungry," she says with a smirk and glides to the next pair to see what their rules are.

"Next rule, Rule Number Four: Men must be served four- no five meals per day by the women." Cooper brainstorms aloud.

"Yeah, that will show Mrs. Hathaway, we won't be hungry or naked!" I quickly jot down our fourth rule. "Okay, Rule number Five: All people must go to school or work five days a week."

"What? That's ridiculous, dude?" Cooper shouts.

"Tone it down, I don't want to live in a stupid, lazy society. We need to learn and work, women don't like stupid men who do nothing." I defend our fifth rule. My daddy isn't workin, but he's not stupid- he's the smartest man I know. He wants to work- he's not lazy at all- he cooks, cleans, and takes care of things for Mama.

"Good point, we should learn and work for the ladies. Okay add your rule."

"What about the sixth and seventh rules?" I ask, hesitantly, because I know Cooper's creative ideas just keep flowin. "We have food, clothes, women who cook and clean for us and men who work- plus no whiskey, what else do we need to cover?"

"Hmmm, dogs- each household should have a dog- that should be rule six. That will make the children in the society happy." Cooper adds excitedly. "We can't have dogs at my house, my mom is allergic."

We don't have a dog and I'm kind of glad- I bet we couldn't afford one now, on the other hand, it would be nice to have a pet to take on long walks and take care of. Mama says we can't bring anything else into the house that eats or poops- there are enough things in the house that eat and poop already.

"Rule Seven: No pooping in public," I shout! Cooper bursts into laughter and nods in agreement as I write our final rule down just in time for the bell to signal that it's time for the next class. I hand our seven rules to Mrs. Hathaway as we walk out of the room and head towards Math class. I hope Julie didn't hear our rules, I bet her rules were normal- but I probably had more fun!

At the end of the day, after math, science, art, Spanish and social studies, the 3:30 p.m. bell finally rings and we are released into the car line to find our way home. As I wait in the line with Cooper, we laugh about our ingenious seven rules from Hathaway's class. "Dude….everyone is gonna love our rules- they only dream of being as cool as us! Hey, my mom is here, later dude." Cooper says as he walks towards his mom's clean white Suburban. She must have washed it today, no one in Memphis has a white car in February.

"Later," I reply- in awe of his shiny, non-dented SUV. As Cooper's mom pulls away, I hear John shout, "Tyler, our ride is here."

Daddy pulls in, in his silver Lexus. "Hey guys, have a good day?" Daddy says as we climb in the back seat. Sarah is perched up front, like always- ear buds in, trying to sing and trying not to listen to anyone else.

"Great day!" John shouts as he crawls across the back seat and I slide in last.

"It was alright, how was your day, Dad?" I ask, knowing he probably doesn't want to talk about it.

"Good, I got the laundry and dishes done, house vacuumed, a couple of resumes e-mailed out and some yard work done. Your Mama will come home to a clean house, when she gets off work tonight, and you boys are not going to mess it up when we get home." Daddy replies in a commanding tone.

That night there was more mumbling after we went to bed. I wonder if Mama and Daddy are talking about her meeting with the principal. Mama said I am not in trouble: that she met with him about something else. Something I don't have to worry about. It makes me wonder and worry, if we'll be able to keep going to St.

Paul. I know it costs money for us to go there and I know things are tight, but I don't want to go anywhere else, my friends are there and the teachers are nice, for teachers. I fit in at St. Paul- well, as much as a nobody can. I have my routine of blending in, sitting quietly, reading or drawing pictures- I can't imagine being an awkward nobody anywhere else.

Chapter Five: More Changes Comin'

At breakfast, Daddy is packing our lunches. Generic creamy peanut butter and strawberry jelly on cheap white bread that tears when you spread the peanut butter on it, a bag of chips and an apple are neatly placed in our lunch boxes. Daddy's been doing the laundry and dishes too. Our lunches are lighter than they used to be. No more Oreos or Twinkies, but that's ok, some people don't even have lunch- so I don't complain about no sweets. Mama says there's starving people in Africa- I bet they don't even have a peanut butter sandwich for lunch.

Some of the kids at school have heavy lunches and they give me stuff on days when they can't eat it all. My friend, Cooper, he never eats his lunch. His medicine makes him not feel very hungry- I wish I had medicine that made me not hungry- Cooper lets me have his cheese crackers and his apple. I feel bad takin other people's food that their Mama's have packed for them, but I don't want them to throw it away either. Food should be eaten, not thrown away and who better than to eat somebody's unwanted food than a nobody- me?

Daddy keeps lookin for jobs, sending resumes in, calling people, but nothing happens. He's at the kitchen table every morning and every evening when we come home, there he sits. He spends more time with us at night, we watch movies together and talk about the books we're reading. Mama is too tired at night anymore, she's been trying to work extra to make ends meet. She took a job at Target stocking shelves in the evenings. By the time she gets home from both of her jobs, she can hardly move. She comes in and sits on the couch with us, asking us about our days and checking on Daddy's job search. She's always so positive, even when she's so tired she can hardly lift her head to watch the movie with us. She will rest her head on Daddy's shoulder. Even in hard times their love shines through. He puts his big strong arm around her and she snuggles in, falling asleep as we finish watching the movie.

One Monday night, we come home, and Daddy tells us that things have gotten pretty tight- as if that was a surprise- but our savings is almost gone and he can't find a job, so things have to be tighter. No birthday parties, brown bag lunches, small dinners, no new shoes or clothes or new anything. We shopped at the Salvation Army when we needed something or more often we would get bags of hand me downs from one of Mama's friends. They had too many clothes, some still with tags on them, and would give them to us.

Daddy says more changes are coming. Mama had gone to my school to talk to the principal, Mr. Wheatley, about my tuition. Mr. Wheatley told Mama we could have a partial scholarship for the rest of this year, but Daddy says that if he doesn't find a job soon we will have to go to public school next year. We will still have to pay part of my tuition for the last few months of school, but with what's left of our savings and Mama working two jobs, we can do it.

The days of Mama working and Daddy staying at home just keep coming. Daddy does more at home so Mama can work a little more. Daddy doesn't cook like mama, but his spaghetti is pretty good. March, April, May, no job for Daddy. Daddy says our savings is gone. Mama opens the bills each day with more dread. Some days she doesn't even open the envelopes, she just stacks them up with the rest. You can see the stress in her face. Her energy and happiness have been zapped. She tries to have a brave face for us, but we're not stupid- she can't fool us. Things can't get tighter- there's nothing left to cut.

Chapter Six: Last Day of School

"Tyler, Tyler, wake up" John shouts two inches from my ear, waking me from a deep sleep. "It's the last day of school, hurry, you don't wanna be late." John is always loud- even when it is morning and I don't want to hear loud. I want quiet- John is so excited for summer, he can't even comprehend quiet. For me- the last day of school is a combination of dread and joy. I am dreading that today is our last day at St. Paul. Since Daddy is still unemployed we won't be able to afford tuition for next year. I've heard all sorts of horror stories about public schools- drugs, beatings, shootings, gangs, and more horrible events that I've only seen on the news. I think John lives in his own little world of happy- he makes friends wherever he goes and he is hoping we go to a school without homework. Mama hasn't told him that all schools have homework, we are saving that for a surprise. Picturing John's face when he finds out that he'll have homework brings me joy.

"I'm up John, beat it." I grumble at him as I wave him away from my bed and sit up. Breathing in, the sweet smell of breakfast drifts up the staircase. For a second, I forget about Daddy not working, having to go to public school and all of the cutbacks we have had the past five months as our savings dwindled along with Mama and Daddy's joy. Mama must be cookin' a special "last day of school" breakfast to help us be cheery. I climb out of bed, slip on my St. Paul uniform for the last time, grab my backpack and slink down the stairs to the kitchen.

"Good morning, Mama, breakfast smells good," I kiss Mama on the cheek as she grabs two warm waffles out of the toaster and places them on a blue square plate and hands it to me. Mama hates having to leave St. Paul just as much as I do- she's made friends with the parents there and trusts the teachers. She knows we are getting a good education and that if John acts up, the teacher will tell her. I don't act up, so there's no worries about me.

"Good morning, Tyler, happy last day of school." Mama says in her soothing voice.

I join Daddy at the table, he's drinking coffee and reading the paper. Sarah is slumped over her plate playing with pieces of waffle and syrup- Miss Drama Queen has been pouting for weeks that she has to leave her friends and her boyfriend, Sean. John bounds down the steps and skips to his chair- his excitement for summer is a little hard to handle amongst those of us feeling sorry for ourselves.

Mama grins as John attacks his waffle with his fork, building a golden cabin before devouring it in one bite.

"Alright, y'all let's get going to school. Put your dishes in the sink and grab your backpacks, I'll meet you at the car." Mama says as she puts the last toasted waffle on Daddy's plate, kisses him on the cheek and grabs her car keys.

John races to the minivan- one shoe on, one shoe in his hand and his backpack slung over his shoulder, syrup still dripping down his chin. Sarah slinks slowly to the passenger seat, head down with a solemn look on her tear stained face. I grab my bag, slip on my high-tops and walk to the van. The drive to school is a quiet one today, Mama drops Sarah off first, then John and me. As Mama pulls up to the front door of St. Paul, John darts out of the car and down the hallway to his classroom. I wave good-bye at Mama and walk to my classroom. As I enter the room, Julie is standing with her friends, chit chatting about summer vacation plans.

"Hey Tyler, where are you going this summer?" Julie asks, as if she really wants to know. She just wants an excuse to tell one more person about the fantastic trip her family is taking.

I take the bait, "Nowhere, we aren't going anywhere this summer, what about you, Julie? What are your summer vacation plans?" I ask, loving that I can just listen and stare at her as she flicks her blonde hair as she talks.

"Oh me? We are going to New Orleans, then taking a cruise to Mexico. We get to parasail, zip line and scuba dive. It's going to be amazing! Have y'all ever been on a cruise, Tyler? You just have to go sometime, we go on one every summer and this one is going to be the BEST!"

"Sounds like fun, Julie. I can't wait to see ...." I cut my sentence short knowing that I won't be here in the fall to see her summer vacation pictures or hear all about her luxurious, over the top vacation. Julie has already spotted another classmate and buzzes off to talk to them.

I wander over to Cooper and the guys as they have a competition to see who can shoot the most paper balls into the trash can before Mr. Malcolm yells at them to stop. Cooper opens up his desk and reveals hundreds of school papers- I'm pretty sure he has papers from August stuffed in there. He and the guys start grabbing and smashing the paper to form balls and shoot them at the trash can. I just smile- there's no trash in my desk and I absolutely don't want Mr. Malcolm to bark at me today. If he gets mad enough he won't let us go to the awards assembly and I don't want to miss it. I should be racking up the awards this year, perfect attendance, honor roll, most handsome 7th grader- okay, so that's not an actual award, but if it was it would have my name on it.

The chaos of happy summer bound 7th graders fills the room- you can almost taste summer, the taste of freedom, sleeping in, swimming all day, sunshine, no homework- it's delicious. The excitement sweeps me away from my pity party for just a moment, until Mr. Malcolm calls our attention to roll call and the morning devotion.

I sit in my desk listening to Mr. Malcolm talk about God and how much He loves us and watches over us and I just think, really? Where's God when my Daddy is lookin for a job? Where's God when the bill collectors make Mama cry? Where's God when I feel like all of our happiness is slipping away? There's no way I can ask Mr. Malcolm where God is, he'll just say that God is everywhere, but I don't feel Him today.

After the awards assembly, John and I meet out front of school to wait for Daddy to pick us up. He pulls in front of the school, driving Mama's red mini-van. John hugs his teacher and waves to his friends.

"See ya next fall, Tyler," Cooper shouts as we walk away.

I just can't bring myself to tell anyone that I'm not comin' back, "Sure, see ya." I tell Cooper good-bye and we climb in the back of the van.

"Hey Daddy, where's your car? Why are you driving Mama's van? Where's Mama?" John gives him the twenty questions as I buckle myself in.

"They repossessed my car today boys, we just couldn't afford it anymore and they took it." I can smell the whiskey on his breath and hear the shaking in his voice, more of Daddy's pride had been stolen as they towed his SUV down the street. The car that he loved to drive, the non-faded, non-smelly car that we weren't allowed to eat in or be dirty in. "Your Mama is at work, we will go pick her up this afternoon."

Daddy pulled out of the car line and pointed the mini-van toward home. We drove home in silence, pure silence. John was sad about leaving his friends, Daddy is sad about losing his car and I'm just sad. I can picture my friends and how excited for summer they were- summer camps and vacations occupied their thoughts, while spending a summer at home with John and Sarah as Daddy struggled with losing his job was on my mind.

Chapter Seven: Good-bye House

June 1st, a day forever etched in my mind as the day our home changed. Mama and Daddy had taken us with them to run some errands. We all piled into the mini-van, since Daddy's car had been taken away last month when we couldn't make the payments anymore. Luckily, our old red mini-van was paid for. No one would take it! It had a "smell" and a squeaky noise that was unique- we had definitely used that van through the years. It had transported us on many family vacations over the years and dropped us off at play dates, sports events, and the movies. I never thought it would become our home.

    We pulled in the driveway that day and there was a sign on the door. When Daddy walked up to read the sign, he saw the padlock. We lost our house. Well, technically it wasn't lost- we knew exactly where it was, it just wasn't ours anymore. It housed all of our treasures, our toys, clothes, anything I thought I could never live without was locked behind that door. Mama sat in the van, motionless- her face showed a combination of fear, anger and hopelessness. Just when I thought her face couldn't look more pale or sad, she would suffer another disappointment, another dream gone by the wayside. Daddy stood in front of our house- the house we grew up in- the house he worked so hard to buy, the house Mama had painted every wall in and sewn custom window coverings for.

He didn't move. For a minute, I thought time had frozen- my parents appeared to resemble statues- we were forever frozen in that sad, angry moment. After what seemed like hours, but was probably just five minutes, Daddy turned around- his swollen eyes solemnly staring at Mama, his cheeks flushed with sorrow. He climbed into the passenger side of the van and Mama started driving.

Sarah, John and I sat silently, no one wanting to be the one to break the silence. Mama drove, no destination, no purpose except to fill time, she just drove and drove.

Finally, Mama pulled into a parking lot of the Memphis Inn and said this would be our home for a little bit- just long enough to get back on our feet, whatever that means. I wonder if I'll ever see my bed again, it was nothing special, but you don't think about how nice something is until you're in a van with your whole family and realize what you have on you is all you have: no toys, no extra clothes, no bed, no books, nothing. We have lots of nothing.

Daddy checked us into a small hotel room, two beds and a cot- one bathroom, one dusty TV, and free Wi-Fi. It's definitely not home- but I guess it will work and it's better than living in the van. Mama and Sarah get one bed, John and I share the other one and Daddy sleeps on the cot. Princess Sarah should let Daddy have the bed, but she would never sleep on cot and Daddy would do anything to make his princess happy.

In the morning Mama and Daddy sit at the little round table in the corner and work on a plan to get some of our things from the house. Seems that most of our things will be sold to pay for our bills, but we will be able to get some clothes and memorabilia out in a few days. I hope they let us have our clean socks, because John's feet are stinky and I can't stand it if he doesn't change his socks for days on end. John wants his DS, but Mama says we only get what we need and we don't NEED a videogame. John argues that he NEEDS it, but he loses; Mama is always right and we don't have room in our new home/van for everything we used to own.

I sit quietly, making a list of the things I "need": underwear, jacket, pants, shorts, socks, shirt, favorite book, backpack, pencils, journal, iPod, snacks, school yearbook, pillow and blanket. Sarah glances over at my list, says you might want your Bible, a toothbrush and some soap. She's right- I need some Jesus and some soap!

Since we had no house and Mama and Daddy got rid of their cell phones, the bill collectors started calling K&H offices where Mama worked. Her boss said it was too disruptive and she was too distracted, so they let Mama go. She's still working a few hours at Target each night, but that's just enough for gas money and the cheap hotel.

The day comes when we can go to the house. We have twenty-four hours to get what we "need" and get out. When they unlock the door to the house, I feel like running in like I'm at Macy's on the Day after Thanksgiving, but the stone face of the man unlocking the door tells me to calm it down. He has probably never lived at the Memphis Inn. Certainly he thinks we're one of those stupid lazy families that refuses to work and pay bills. He's stupid. He doesn't know us- just thinks he does. He doesn't know how hard Daddy worked or how badly Daddy wants a new job. He has no clue what a hard worker my Mama is or that no matter how many jobs she had, the mountain of bills would just never disappear.

Mama has us all organize our things as rapidly as possible- box up the things we want to put in storage and we each get a duffle bag to keep in the van. Have you ever tried to put your life into an Adidas sports bag? Being a 12 year old boy- I am not real sentimental, but there are things that make me feel good and things I want with me. Mama says clean socks are more important than comic books and to make sure I get everything on my list. There's no room for my guitar, or John's basketball or Sarah's extensive OPI nail polish collection.

Daddy loads the boxes in the van and makes several trips to the storage shed- not sure how long our stuff will be locked up, or how long we can pay for it to be there. Mama tags the rest of our things to sell and after working all day at packing, tagging and laughing at memories, the stone face man comes in and tells us it's time to lock up again. Saying good-bye is not easy when you don't know what you're saying hello to.

Closing that door for the final time, was like an ending to a part of our family story that I didn't want to end. It's like at the conclusion of a movie when everything goes black and you sit in the theater just wondering what's going to happen next and then the giant monster appears out of nowhere and tears you to shreds. The fear from saying good-bye to our home was eating me up, wishing I could just be shredded and not have to face whatever was coming next.

As we slowly pull away from our house for the last time, I can hear Mama's breath shaking. I look away so not to see her tears fall down her cheeks. That night at the Memphis Inn, we all agreed to go to bed early. I don't know if it was exhaustion, depression or fear but I fell asleep to the shaky breaths of the five of us as we ended the day.

Chapter Eight: Nana's House

The next morning we are awoken by Mama cheerily asking, "Ready for a summer vacation? We are going to Nana's! Get up, let's go!" She is smiling, but her words are shaky and hesitant, like she's trying to convince herself to be positive in the face of fear and uncertainty. I grasp on to the fear and empathize. How is going to Nana's going to be fun? Does she know that we are without a house, without money, without hope? We check out of the Memphis Inn, for now, and load the mini-van again. Once settled, Sarah sits unmoving, the fear has frozen her too. She stares straight ahead, at the back of the driver seat, no tears, no smiles, just fear.

John, on the other hand, grasps onto the fake positivity in Mama's voice and hollers, "Yippee!" as Sarah and I roll our eyes at his enthusiasm.

"Don't you have to work, Mama?" I ask, but she just shakes her head no.

"They don't need me at Target anymore. They are cutting back and can't afford to keep me." Mama's voice trails.

I wonder when things will get bad enough that Mama and Daddy can't afford me anymore. I make a mental note to not be "expensive." A list of don'ts forms in my head: don't eat too much, don't ask for anything, don't look hungry or tired and don't look disposable.

Daddy cuts in, "We'll take a little break and hang out with Nana for a while and then we'll get back on our feet. Let's focus on fun times with family for a bit." I can tell that he and Mama are worried and I don't think they've told Nana why we're coming, but I'm happy to leave the hotel for a while. We could use some fun family time.

The road winds on and on as we navigate through Arkansas to Nana's house in Hot Springs. I stare out the window at the changing scenery- beautiful trees, blue skies, dirt brown cliffs, and the road winds on, curving this way and that like a nervous snake, not sure where to hide. I imagine we are taking an exotic vacation to the mountains. When I was younger and liked John and Sarah, we went to Mountain Home, Arkansas to camp one summer. We camped in a tent and would wake up to the fog drifting off the lake, it was the most beautiful scene. My thoughts are like that fog right now, appearing heavy and slowly dissolving as the sun comes up.

Three hours later, Daddy pulls the van into Nana's curved driveway. There stands Nana, wearing a blue floral dress and purple Nike's in true cool Nana style. She's standing next to her white picket fence waving and smiling at us. Her dog, Bentley, a gray/white miniature poodle is standing at her feet, yipping, to notify her that there are strangers approaching. As the van slows to a stop, Mama leans between the driver and passenger seats and whispers, "Don't tell Nana about staying in a hotel or about moving out of the house, or that our stuff is in storage- we will tell her, just not right now."

"Yes, ma'am," we all respond. I'm not sure why we can't tell Nana, I'm sure she would help us- although, none of us really know what we need- or why exactly we need help, but staying at Nana's will be a nice distraction from worrying and Nana has nice comfy beds and homemade food for all of us. A big improvement from the complimentary cereal from the hotel that we'd been filling our pockets with for lunch and dinner.

Uncertain of what we are supposed to say or how we are supposed to act, we prepare to pile out of the van and intrude on Nana's perfectly groomed lawn with the beautiful rose bushes and colorful pansies.

The van door slides open and John explodes out of the van and into Nana's arms- almost toppling her over. Nana is a petite lady standing about 5'3" and John's energy is about twelve feet tall, in his four and a half foot tall body. Sarah grabs her bag, "Hi Nana," she says as she kisses her on the cheek, ear buds still in, and makes her way to the bonus room us kids usually stay in. I help Daddy grab the rest of the bags and haul them in to the house. Mama and Nana share a long embrace- we haven't seen Nana since Christmas- since before our season of loss, losing jobs, losing the house, losing normal. I'm sure Nana can tell something is wrong- she knows everything. Bentley runs around in circles as everyone invades her yard and home. He is yipping and running and jumping around like a crazy jumping bean!

Mama and Nana go straight to the kitchen to start cooking dinner. Bentley, the tiny guard dog, follows Nana to the kitchen. Daddy goes to the living room and picks up the remote, flipping straight to the sports channel to watch golf. Sarah is still up in the bonus room listening to her music and trying to sing along. John goes to the backyard to play and I decide to sit out on the patio, watching John weave back and forth with the old soccer ball he grabbed from Nana's garage. His playfulness and energy seem unaffected by our "situation," like he doesn't even care or worry that we don't have a house to call home, that all of our stuff is in storage with the exception of five backpacks of clothes and our most favorite items. I stare out at Nana's backyard- wondering when we will get to unpack our clothes for good- or at least for more than a couple of nights.

    Sitting on the patio, I listen intently to Mama and Nana as they converse. I try to be invisible, unseen and unheard as I lean towards the screen door trying to catch Mama's words as they fall slowly from her mouth and into Nana's caring ears. I can hear Nana asking Mama about work, Daddy's job, the Lexus that we used to have, our precious Lutheran school, our house and all of the things we have lost since Christmas. But, Nana doesn't know those things aren't ours anymore, she's clueless to the loss that we've experienced since Christmas, or so I think she is. Nana is a good listener and she must suspect something or she wouldn't know exactly what questions to ask Mama to get her to open up and be honest with her about our visit.

Nana begins, "Dear, how did you and Ben both get vacation at the same time? It's been years since y'all could all visit me as a family."

"Umhummm," Mama agrees. "It's been a long time, Mom."

"Honey, is something wrong? You have sleep all over your face and the kids look tired too."

I can hear Nana asking Mama, "How's work going? Is it keeping you busy?" I see Mama nod and shrug her shoulders as she stirs the pot over the stove. "Well, what about Ben's job, did he get the promotion he's always wanted?"

I see Mama look away, "Not exactly, we both lost our jobs. Ben lost his in January and just last week K & H made cutbacks including letting me go. We lost the house, the Lexus, the kids have lost their school, most of our stuff is being sold to pay bills and the rest is in a tiny storage unit in Memphis." Mama's voice was shaky and began to trail off.

Nana wrapped her arms around her and held her while she cried. I looked back at John, running with the soccer ball as if everything was A-Okay. Tears began to well up in my eyes as I thought about all the things we have lost, but they quickly disappeared as Daddy joined me on the back patio. I turn and secretly wipe my eyes with sleeve of my t-shirt, such a John move, but I don't want Daddy to see me crying. I'm the strong one, even though I don't feel very strong, I feel lost.

"Hey, Sport, what's going on out here?" Daddy asks nonchalantly.

"John's playing and I'm watching- Mama and Nana are cookin and cryin. Daddy, how long are we stayin' here?" I ask, hoping he has an answer.

Daddy avoids my question and my eyes, he looks over at John as he runs around the backyard, "Let's play soccer with John, come on Tyler, Dad versus you two- see if y'all can beat this old man." Daddy grabs my hand and pulls me up out of my chair to help me stand up. John and I make a good team- he's quick and can get right past Dad to shoot the ball into the goal and I can block any shots Daddy tries to make!

"Hey, can I join?" Sarah yells from the backdoor. The princess has decided to join us. It's a very rare occasion that Sarah doesn't have her earbuds in, she must be sick. She's probably sick of being alone- when you're alone you can't help but think, at least when you are running around and playing, your mind can have a reprieve from the negativity and worry that weigh you down.

"Sure, come on!" Dad waves Sarah onto his team. We played for what seemed like forever, laughing, pushing, and running around Nana's backyard like the good ole days when we were little and would all play together. The good ole days were so long ago. I'm not sure when the last time I saw Daddy truly smile was, hearing his full and hearty laugh as John would wiz by him with the ball was comforting to me. A reminder that we can still be happy, we are still a family that loves each other. We are also a family that loves to win!

"S-c-o-r-e," John yells, as he makes the final goal of the night. As we all turn towards the house we see Mama and Nana with their arms around each other admiring our togetherness. John runs across the yard, holding his pointer finger in the air, announcing, "NUMBER ONE! We are number one!" A chorus of *We are the Champions* arises as I chase John toward the patio.

"Dinner time," Mama announces, her smile a little brighter than it had been in weeks. Being with her mama makes her worry lines disappear, at least for a while.

Sitting around the dining room table at Nana's house brings back so many happy memories of Christmases, Easters, birthdays and family reunions. Mama is an only child, so most holidays we come to Nana's house and it's just us. When Papa was alive he would tell jokes and play with us kids. He died two years ago from lung cancer. We came around a lot that year, during Nana's season of loss, to comfort her. It's only appropriate that we would come back here to Nana's during our season of loss too.

Nana and Mama outdid themselves in the kitchen: meatloaf with bacon on top, Nana's home grown green beans that she cans each year, peaches and fresh bread. Nana taught Mama all she knows about cooking and feeding a family. They spent a lot of time cooking together through the years and this meal was like a dose of much needed medicine for our family. I can't remember the last time I was full, or the last time I truly enjoyed dinner. We didn't have to be quiet, Daddy didn't have whiskey, (that was one of the things cut out right before we lost the house), and we laughed, told jokes, and threw bread across the table when someone requested a slice of the warm yeasty goodness!

Climbing the soft carpeted stairs to the bonus room after dinner, our stomachs were full, but more importantly, so were our hearts. Nana has the best medicine, love. Her home has always radiated love and generosity. John, Sarah and I stayed up late playing board games, UNO, Sorry and Monopoly, until our bodies just couldn't stay awake any longer.

As I lay down to sleep, I can feel my face smiling- something it's not done without force in a long time. How good this feels, but I start to wonder, to worry, how long can we be happy before life hits us again? How long will Nana take care of us? John fell asleep immediately upon snuggling into his sleeping bag on the futon and Sarah put her earbuds in, of course, and listened to her music as she drifted off to sleep. I lay on the futon next to John ignoring his snorts, counting my blessings and trying to not count my worries.

The next two weeks at Nana's was blissful. Nana treated us to so many fun activities, I almost forgot we were poor. We took long walks, hiked through Hot Springs National Park, golfed with Nana's friends, shopped, raced go karts, zip lined, made homemade ice cream, and played board games- sometimes Nana would even let us win. Mama did a lot of cooking, that was her stress relief and Daddy played games with us in the evenings after working on his laptop from the couch all day. He would search for jobs, send e-mails, fill out applications and keep trying to find employment. At dinner each night Daddy would update us on his progress for the day and we would pray together that he would get an interview soon. Nana is an encourager, she would end each prayer with an affirmative Amen and reassure Daddy that he would hear something soon from one of the many companies he had contacted about work.

"Ben will get a job soon and we will move out, Mom" Mama would tell Nana, "We don't want to be a nuisance, or overstay our welcome."

"My house is your house, you are my daughter and we are family, you are always welcome," Nana would reply. Nana means what she says- we are family and she will always welcome us into her home, but Daddy is our provider and he is not going to let someone else support his family for very long. Daddy is determined, more than ever to be the man of the house so to speak and go back to work. I'm ready for our old normal again, I love being at Nana's, her food is delicious and having Bentley around to play with is entertaining, but I long for our own space again, a place we can unpack the few belongings we have and call home.

Monday night at dinner, Daddy declares he has an announcement to make, some good news. We all stop eating and chatting as Daddy proudly begins, "I heard back from a company in Memphis and they have a management position opening next week.

They have asked me to come for an interview. The job sounds great and I think I have a good chance of getting it!"

We all clap and hoot and holler as if we just won a million dollars!

"I told you, you could do it, Ben," Nana kisses him on the cheek, "this is a cause for celebration." Nana brings out a homemade angel food cake. Sarah jumps up to get the whipped cream and berries from the refrigerator and sets them down next to Daddy.

"When is your interview?" Mama asks, calculating when we will need to return to Memphis.

"They asked me to come in Thursday to meet with the interview committee, if I get it, then I will start right away Friday morning." Daddy replies before shoving a fork fool of spongy cake, sweet cream and a slice of red juicy strawberry into his mouth. His grin doesn't even straighten when he chews.

"Great! We will leave Wednesday, then. We have enough money left to get a hotel room for a couple of nights and once you start we can start looking for an apartment," Mama plans out loud.

The smiles around the table could illuminate a small city with their excitement and energy. Happiness feels foreign and wonderful at the same time, however the weight of worries creeps into my joy filled mind. "Can John and I go to St. Paul in the fall? Will Sarah go back to her high school? Where will we live? What about Daddy's car?"

Mama's gentle voice answers my worried inquiries, "God has a plan, Tyler, I don't know the answers to your questions, but I do know that we will be okay and Daddy will take care of us."

Her voice is calm and almost convincing. I don't want to go back to the tiny hotel room where we all sleep in the same room, but I do want Daddy to get this position so that we can have a home again, even if it is an apartment.

Tuesday is filled with gathering our things and packing the van. We always leave Nana's with more than we came with and this trip is no different. Along with the toys and clothes that our bags were filled with, our hearts were full of happiness and hope- something our hearts were devoid of two weeks ago. We play more games and enjoy our last day together before our return home.

Wednesday morning is a mixture of emotions, excitement for Daddy's interview, sadness to leave the love of Nana's house and worry about what lies ahead. Nana packed a cooler of goodies, homemade cookies, Cokes, bottles of water, ham and cheese sandwiches and pears for our drive back to Memphis. Sarah sprawls across the back bench, earbuds in and music on. Daddy places the cooler in between John and my seats in the middle of the van, we get in and immediately go for the Hershey's bars Nana had put in a baggie at the top of the cooler.

Nana and Mama share a long embrace. I observe Mama as she kisses Nana on the cheek one last time and Nana slips a small green wad into her hand. Mama thanks Nana and slides into the passenger seat, putting the folded green bills in the console and closes the door. Daddy thanks Nana one last time for her hospitality and starts the van.

As we slowly back out of Nana's driveway, Mama wipes away a few tears and waves at the petite lady standing in her yard surrounded by flowers, green grass and Bentley yipping and running. Nana's house gets smaller as we drive away, Nana and Bentley turn and go inside the now quiet house. Everything seems quiet after we leave.

We drive back towards Memphis enjoying the beautiful sunshine that June brings and the gorgeous foliage that marks our path home. I am excited for this new adventure, but I am not excited to stay in the tiny hotel room again. At least this time we have a pool to swim in and there will be free hot breakfast in the morning- I love the biscuits and gravy that hotels sometimes serve with their continental breakfast.

Chapter Nine: Return to Memphis

Thursday morning Daddy wakes up early to shower, shave and put his shirt and tie on for his interview. Mama and Daddy talk as if we are all still asleep. I can hear Mama tell Daddy that he will do great, he is dressed to impress and someone would be foolish to not hire such a smart, handsome man. I am trying to bury my head in my covers before their conversation gets overly affectionate.

Ready for his interview, Daddy kisses Mama and leaves. After Daddy leaves, Mama sits at the circular table in the corner of the hotel room, stirring her coffee and breathing deeply. It looks like she's praying, eyes closed, slow breathes, just praying. I close my eyes too and pray, "Dear Jesus, Please let my Daddy get this job. Please don't let us lose anything else. Thank you for listening. Amen."

I look up and Mama's eyes are open. She sees me too and smiles.

"Time for breakfast, Tyler. Help me wake Sarah and John up so we can get dressed and get something to eat."

After breakfast John, Sarah and I go down to the hotel pool to waste time and enjoy the water. June in Memphis is warm, you don't do much outside in Memphis once it gets too hot, unless you are in a pool!

John, Sarah and I enjoy the pool time, swimming, floating, and splashing, when Mama isn't looking, and just relaxing. I look over and see Daddy come in, smile gone, motioning for Mama to join him away from the pool, away from our ears. His face does not contain the hope and excitement it did earlier this morning. I look away hoping that if I don't see him tell Mama bad news, that it just won't be true. Maybe he's trying to trick Mama by looking sad, but really he has great news. Mama comes back to the pool area, her face matches Daddy's solemn look of despair. There was no trick, just truth. Daddy didn't get the job. Disappointment hits us as we all share the same look, no words, just a look that says, "What now?" and no one knows the answer.

After we return to our hotel room and get changed, we sit staring at the walls, not sure what to do next. I hear Mama and Daddy talking about money. I can tell, because their voices change when their conversation is centered on money. It's a serious tone of voice, with a dash of fear and a trembling of uncertainty.

"We have enough money for one more night here, then we are out. My mom gave us just enough to help us for a short while." Mama says.

Daddy just stares at her, nodding in agreement. Mama is the planner, Daddy is the provider and we kids are the workers- chore doers. Mama still plans, but I don't know how Daddy is going to provide for us. Daddy replies to Mama with a sense of false confidence, "We will figure it out, together." In that instant I know that the future path we take may be hard, but Mama and Daddy will take care of us. They have never failed us.

The next morning I awake to Mama organizing and packing the belongings that we have with us. Folding our clothes that she had washed by hand the day before and hung to dry around the shrinking hotel room. Daddy is looking over the newspaper that had been laid outside our room door early this morning. We all awake and shuffle down to the breakfast room, filling up on biscuits and gravy, fluffy yellow eggs, waffles, bananas and yogurt. I see Mama place a couple of boxes of cereal in her purse for later. After breakfast, with full stomachs, we load our bags into the van, Daddy pays our balance at the front desk and we get settled into our new home- the van.

Chapter Ten: Nowhere

Have you ever been headed for nowhere? Literally, not knowing where you are going. It's a beautiful June day in Memphis; sunshiny, warm, no work or school to negate what we have to accomplish, yet, here we sit in a well-used minivan with all of our dearest possessions and we have no idea what is next. Mama and Daddy share a confused look and Daddy begins to drive.

"Where are we goin' Daddy?" John asks from the middle seat.

"Not sure, John, let's see where the road takes us today." Daddy's voice has a hint of fake optimism and mystery with a dash of uncertainty, like goulash, you never know exactly what's in it, but it looks good enough to try.

Sarah sits behind me in the van, earbuds in, of course, but this time her nose is pressed against the window as we drive downtown in Memphis. I press my nose against the window, too and we sit and look. We drive along I-40 watching Memphis as we get closer to its heart. St. Jude Research Hospital, the Pyramid, old churches, the Mississippi River, the Redbirds stadium, a billboard with a big picture of Elvis, and a cluster of office buildings and shops welcome us to downtown Memphis. Daddy parks the van near the river and we pile out of it. Mama takes out the cereal from the hotel and fills her purse with a few snacks left over from Nana's house and we begin our walk without a purpose.

The river offers a cool breeze as we saunter next to it, crossing the long red bridge to wander the Mud Island River Park and splash in the fountain. Many Memphians enjoy the cool of the fountain in the miniature "gulf" at the end of the river. Looking around, I wonder where the other children live- how many of them parked their house to come play in the water? I notice women with Coach bags and matching sandals- definitely not homeless- kids with parents watching them closely, some with parents whom are playing on their phones not even noticing how far their kids have walked away.

Mama and Daddy got rid of their fancy phones, had to sell them before we went to Nana's, so we'd have gas money. Daddy went to the neighborhood store and got a prepaid phone so that he could be reached for interviews, but it's not a phone that we can play games on or anything. Just something to use for emergencies and job opportunities. His phone didn't ring at all yesterday or today. Opportunity is not knocking or ringing at his door.

It must be about lunch time as families unfold blankets and display picnic baskets full of sandwiches, juicy watermelon and the like. Mama pulls out five granola bars, an apple and a knife from her purse. We each take a granola bar as Mama slices the apple and doles out a slice to each of us. Sarah is used to eating small portions, she's always worried about her weight, but John inhales his granola bar, hungrily hoping for more. "That's it," Mama says, as she offers John half of her granola bar and the last piece of apple. Mama would give us her last bite of anything- no matter what.

Sarah and I know not to whine, to appreciate everything that is given to us, but John is still learning how to be grateful. "Mama, I'm still hungry," he moans. Mama shakes her head and motions for

John to go back to the fountain to play. She refills a water bottle at the drinking fountain and relaxes in the shade of a tree near the fountain, watching John play. Daddy sits behind Mama, as she leans on him and Sarah and I sit next to the fountain dangling our feet in the cool water.

"Where do you think we will sleep?" Sarah asks me, looking the other way to try to hide her worry.

"Maybe over there," I half-jokingly point over by the tree that Mama and Daddy sit under. I really don't know where we are going to sleep, or what our next meal will be. The snacks Nana gave us will be gone in a few days, sooner if John gets to them, and I know we are out of money for a hotel. I've heard about homeless shelters, we used to collect coats and things for a shelter when we attended St. Paul, but I never thought about needing to find one for us.

Mama made us volunteer at a homeless kitchen once, to serve lunch after a church service and I remember thinking to myself that there were no kids. It never struck me as weird until now, what happens to kids when they don't have a home? Why weren't they at the shelter, in line for lunch? Surely we are not the first family in Memphis to end up on the streets.

The day continues on, families come and go and we just keep splashing and relaxing, with nowhere to go. The shade of the trees and the nearness of the Mighty Mississippi provide a much needed coolness in the middle of the afternoon. As evening approaches more picnic baskets open, it must be time for dinner. Daddy counts the few bills he has in his pockets and we decide to walk back towards where we parked the van earlier in the day.

Once we return to the van, Mama scrounges through the snack bag and comes up with a few morsels of deliciousness, commonly known as Doritos. Not exactly a healthy meal, but we don't really care- we used to beg for Mama to let us eat Doritos for dinner and she always made us have healthy food. Maybe being homeless does have its perks.

After a quickly eaten dinner of Doritos, we once again walk along the river, enjoying the sunset and observing the many couples walking hand in hand along the waters' edge. Mama and Daddy walk together with their arms around each other and John, Sarah and

I walk behind them like ducklings following wherever their Mama leads them. We pass by a few benches down by the river, occupied by men holding paper bag covered bottles, singing tunes I don't recognize. There's a lady leaned up against a tree in a park, talking out loud, but no one is near her. Part of me wants to know who she is talking to and another part of me wants to move as far away as possible from the lady talking to her invisible friends. I wonder if she hears them answer her or if she notices how people make a point to walk five feet in the opposite direction to avoid being near her. How long has she been sitting there? Is that her home? How long before I start talking out loud to myself? I bet John goes crazy first- he's already half way there. Sarah walks faster, to catch up to Mama and Daddy and get far away from the people making their home in the park.

Finally, it is dark and we walk back to where the van has been parked for the day. Without a word, we all climb in the van, recline the seats that are able to recline and nestle into our "beds" for the night. The van is warm from being parked in the sun all day, so Daddy runs the air conditioning for a minute, then shuts off the van and rolls down the windows to allow the evening breeze to blow through the van.

"Get some sleep, I'll stay up for a while to keep us safe," Daddy whispers to Mama as he gently kisses her cheek and keeps watch while we all try to allow sleep to take our concerns away.

It must have gotten cool enough in the night for Daddy to roll up the windows and fall asleep himself, as when we awoke all the windows were rolled up and Daddy was snoring. Mama presses her finger to her lips to signal us to be quiet, so as to not wake Daddy. Who knows when he finally fell asleep?

Past summers have been filled with family vacations, movies, board games, trips to the neighborhood parks, hikes through Shelby Farms and the like. Mama would work part time in the summers and Sarah would watch us or our neighbor lady, Ruby, would keep an eye on us to make sure we didn't blow up the house. This summer, there will be none of that. Waking up in the mini-van parked down by the Mississippi River, I realize that this summer will not be one that I want to remember- in fact, if I could not be present in this moment that would be ideal.

Mama tries her hardest to give us fun experiences. Daddy drops us off at the zoo on Tuesday afternoons since it's free, and he goes door to door to different restaurants and stores trying to get a job. Mama had gotten a free membership to the Pink Palace museum for the summer, before we were homeless, so we go there many days- it's air conditioned and the bathrooms are nice. Mama takes us to the family restroom when no one is looking to wash us up- taking a "bath" in a museum with thin paper towels, in front of your Mama, brother and sister brings a new level of humility to this shy teenage boy. We all turn towards the walls, so we don't see each other, but it's still humiliating. Sometimes we take turns, Mama and Sarah go first, then John and me, but it depends on how busy the museum is.

No matter where we spend the day, Daddy picks us up each evening. He always has the same story to tell. His perseverance is dwindling with each application he fills out. It's getting harder to apply for jobs the longer we are without an official address- red van parked by river- apparently isn't registered with the post office. Some days Daddy can get cleaned up in a public restroom before going out to apply, but still a paper towel cleaning isn't the same as a house shower. Some of the store managers have mentioned Daddy's smell or wrinkled clothes, just one more twist of the knife during his unemployment journey.

One Sunday morning, as we were walking, Mama noticed a beautiful old church was starting their weekly service, so we walked in and sat down on the back pew, hoping to be filled with some hope and not noticed. During the greeting time at the beginning of the service, a few people came and shook Mama and Daddy's hands, but most would turn around after getting close enough to smell us and wouldn't look us in the eyes. We could hear whispers as they walked away from us. I'm not sure what they said, but I doubt it was pleasant. We didn't return to church after that.

Chapter Eleven: Back to School

Don't judge a book by its cover, or a kid by their clothes or a family by their home. Don't judge me. It's August, the first day of school. Well, really school started a week ago, but when you live on the streets, sometimes you don't know what day it is. So, John, Sarah and I started school today. You know how everyone has the "first day of school" pictures of them in their first day of school clothes, with their new backpacks, new shoes, new pencils, new everything? Well, that's not us. We were lucky to still have our backpacks from last year and we found some used shoes in the dumpster by our "house," but our clothes are old, our pencils were "borrowed" from the library and there's no cute picture of us lined up, ready to go to school. No first day of school smile from us.

Instead, we have our old stuff on our backs as we trek into school a week late. We aren't the only late comers, lots of kids didn't know school started last week. I guess that's common at my new school. At our old school, everyone knew when school was starting and everyone was excited to see their old friends. All of the moms would walk the kids in and take a billion pictures of us as we saw our friends again and met our teacher.

I can imagine how perfect Julie looks on her first day of school- smooth blonde hair, precisely pressed school uniform shirt and skirt- as she begins her first day of 8th grade. I can almost hear her talking to Chelsea and Shelby about her summer cruise while

Cooper and the boys rehash their summer full of hoops and swimming at Cooper's pool.

The only new thing for us this year will be friends, if we make any. Our new school is different. It is darker, poorer, and full of the unknown. New things are full of uncertainties and fear. Will people know where we live? Will we get "caught" being homeless? Will someone make fun of me? Will my wrinkled clothes offend anyone? This is the first time that John and I will have to go to different schools, his elementary school is just down the street from the middle school, though, so I drop him off first and then continue on to the large, mysterious building ahead.

Walking into Roosevelt Middle School, I am greeted by a not so cheerful secretary, "Name? Grade? Address? Parent's name?"

Tyler Smith, 8th grade, address? Um, let me see, we just moved, can I bring it to you tomorrow? My mama is Sandra Smith and my daddy is Ben."

"First thing tomorrow, I need your address or you can't come to school, ya hear? Here's your pass, go to room 23, Mr. Bellows' homeroom, he will get you your list of classes and locker number. Have a nice day."

"Thanks ma'am." I say, trying not to look nervous about the address and folding up the piece of paper for my parents to sign.

Mr. Bellows has already taken role, and adds me to the list for hot lunch. It's free here, the whole school gets free lunch, not just the poor kids, but everyone. If I get here early enough, I get free breakfast too. Two hot meals, awesome! I bet the other kids aren't as excited about free scrambled eggs or oatmeal, but to me, it's heaven. It's food that hasn't been thrown away.

Looking around the classroom I notice that everyone, except me, is wearing khaki pants and a blue polo shirt. Mr. Bellows informs me that this school has a dress code and hands me a piece of paper with the dress code rules listed on it. Since it's the beginning of the year, most everyone still looks clean- I didn't know about the dress code, so we will have to see what we can find tonight. I'm pretty sure I have a pair of Khaki pants in my duffle bag, I'm not sure if they fit, but they'd be better than wearing jeans, I guess. I wonder if John has a dress code too- I'm pretty sure high schools don't have dress codes around here, so Sarah should be okay in her normal clothes. Hopefully, the Salvation Army will have something for John and me. If we can't afford it, we can go into the changing room and put the clothes on under our regular clothes. Mama doesn't like to steal and neither do I, but when you are desperate you do things you never thought you would.

Next, Mr. Bellows tells the girl next to me, Sydney, to go show me where my locker is and help me use my lock. My luck, she's cute and super nice. She hands me my lock and my locker number and escorts me down the hallway. My very own locker, my very own space. To some kids it's just a place to store their books and notebooks, but to me it's like the best thing- I have a place that's mine that I can put my very own things in. I stack my half used notebooks up and slam the door. My space!

The second best thing about my day is meeting Sydney. She reminds me of Julie, but with dark hair. She's beautiful and kind. Her smile tells me I could open up to her, but my mind tells me to keep hiding my secret. The other kids in my classes seem cool too. It's a lot like St. Paul, just bigger. The boys huddle in one corner of the room and the girls gather in the other corner- occasionally a paper ball would fly from the boys side and land on a girl. I didn't feel like I could join the boy's huddle on my first day, so I sat near them, just like I used to at St. Paul- close enough to hear their conversation but far enough way to not intrude. Every few minutes, Sydney would flick her hair over her shoulder and shoot me a smile- I pretended to look away, as if I was not closely observing her every move.

The rest of the day was just like my old school. Sydney is in three of my other classes, so she walked with me when she could, to help show me around. The teachers seem nice, I got a textbook at each class and a little bit of homework- we did most of the work in class, so we wouldn't have to take our books home.

After school, I wait for John at the corner in between our two schools. He exits the school, with Mama by his side. Apparently, John didn't do a very good job at hiding our homelessness, he got nervous and started to cry when they asked him about our address- I knew I should have taken him myself. The school called Mama and Daddy, so Mama went to the school to get things sorted out. I think she has it settled for now, but the school seems suspicious. Mama says they will be assigning a social worker to the case if they are still suspicious, but hopefully that won't go very far.

Chapter Twelve: Hunger Pains

"Sit up, pay attention, this isn't nap time" Mrs. Washington, the math teacher, says.

That's all I hear, day after day. Same song, same tune, same angry smile. Her eyes say that she wants me to learn, but her voice just annoys me. I'm tired- physically tired, no, exhausted. Sleep doesn't come easy to me at home, it runs around my head, like a child playing hide-and-go-seek, but I never find it. When I do finally get close enough to catch it, it disappears again.

Mrs. Washington's voice drones on and on, like a sweet lullaby. I begin to drift off into a warm world of …….. "Tyler, Tyler, wake-up child." Oh man, caught again. I would listen better, learn better, if I could. But, sometimes I just can't.

No, it's not nap time- it's school time, I get it. School time to Mrs. Washington is learning, sitting up straight, saying "yes ma'am." School time to me is warm and predictable. A place to rest. A place to stop chasing dreams and let them come to me. A place to feel safe. A place to eat.

At lunch, the lady in charge, Mrs. Nancy, is always givin' me an extra helping of mashed potatoes when no one else is looking- she says she's gonna put some meat on my bones. I don't mind- most days lunch is the only meal I eat. I'm too tired to get to school early enough for the free breakfast. So, those extra potatoes are delicious to me. They taste like love- even if they are from a box.

On days when I feel like talkin to people, I sit by the girls at the lunch table- they always talk a lot and Sydney gives me her extra snack cake. I say thank you and shove it in my pocket for my sister, just in case she's hungry too. Sarah is super smart and works hard in high school. She works so hard, she doesn't even have time to eat lunch most days. She says you stand in line for most of your break and in high school you only get twenty minutes for lunch anyway, so she just eats when she really needs to and some days she devours the snack cake I get for her and other days, we split it. She always lets me take the bigger half and we sit on a curb, snacking and talking. We eat real slowly so it seems like we are full- even if on the inside we are still empty, still hungry. Still wanting more, but happy to be empty together.

Have you ever been hungry? So hungry you can't think straight. Your stomach doesn't even growl anymore, because it knows no one will answer. I don't mean just stomach hungry, I mean hungry for things you want so deep inside you- you don't even know if they exist, except on T.V.

Hungry for food. Hungry for attention. Hungry for clothes without holes. Hungry for parents that don't fight. Hungry for sleep.

Hungry people don't say, "I'm hungry." Truly hungry people show it in their eyes- their look, you can hear it in their voice- see it in the way they strut in line at the food bank.

"You are what you eat," kids say- well, then I guess I'm nothing.

NOTHING

A mistake- or as my mama says, a happy oops. Well, she don't always seem so happy to have another mouth to feed. Another reason to dive through Memphis dumpsters. Mama would say, "God don't make no mistakes, Tyler. You are somebody." I wish I could believe her, but my hunger kicks in and reminds me that I'm empty. Too empty to be "somebody." Maybe just once, Mama's God made a mistake and named it Tyler.

I miss the days when my stomach was full of pancakes and John and I went to private school. The kids there seemed to share that same full stomach, happy family feeling. Now….now, we are the pale kids mixed in with a sea full of brown, same, but different. Everyone thinks we are the "rich" kids, just because we are lighter and our khaki's don't have holes yet. They don't see the hunger in our eyes, they can't look past our blonde hair.

One day in October, during fall break, Mama and Daddy took us behind the McDonald's to scavenge for dinner. Dumpster diving is a talent, an art that we have unfortunately mastered. After scavenging all over the city we have found which restaurants have the best "trash" and when they throw it all out. Timing is very important- you want to get to the goodies before the rats or the other homeless people, you also want to get there before the bathroom trash is thrown on top of it. Opening up the dumpster, I really missed Daddy's spaghetti and Mama's meatloaf, I even miss ramen noodles and Macaroni & Cheese, but when I found a half-eaten cheeseburger, no pickle, I knew I had hit the jackpot. I took a bite and then carefully wrapped up my treasured food and tucked it discreetly away in my coat pocket like the others did, so we wouldn't be caught. When it's time to eat, I will savor every morsel, knowing it could keep my empty stomach from growling for the night. The good thing about not eating very much is that your stomach doesn't need much to be full. It's easier to fill up a stomach that's not used to eating.

On school days John and I get lunch each day and then scavenge for dinner, but on the weekends or on holidays when we don't have school, we just get one meal- if you can call it that. Mama will take us to search for food once a day. Hunger makes me want to go school. School lunch food is better than someone else's trash.

Chapter Thirteen: Winter

Snow Day- No School, Most kids love snow days, well here in Memphis, it's really an Ice Day, but it's the same thing, NO SCHOOL! To me, I'd rather be in school. It's warm, they have breakfast and lunch for us and Sydney and I get to talk. Sydney is so much nicer than John or Sarah to talk to. I try not to talk too long to her, so she doesn't start to ask too many questions, but it's nice to ask her questions and hear about her life. Her family lives down the street from the school in a tiny blue house, but at least it's warm. She has a brother and sister too, they are both younger and she has to take care of them while her mama works at the neighborhood grocery store. Her daddy left when her sister was a baby, so it's just the four of them. Today, Sydney's probably cuddled up with her siblings, watching movies and eating warm oatmeal. They probably get to go play in the ice and then return to a nice warm home.

Seeing other kids playing in the snow makes me miss having a home, when we could slip and slide in our front yard, make snow angels and have snowball fights. Then when you can't feel your toes anymore and your fingers are purple, Mama calls you in with her sing-songy voice and you go in your nice warm house and drink delicious hot cocoa topped with miniature marshmallows.

Snow days without a home are lonely. You fight to get warm- snow and ice aren't fun when you're frozen to your very core. Your only pair of gloves are thin and holy. Your flimsy shoes keep letting the snow seep in and soak your frozen toes. It's a cold that never seems to thaw.

Today, Daddy stands on the street corner to try to get some help, he says. We stand behind the sidewalk- not too close to the street, but Mama says we aren't going to leave Daddy out there alone either. He holds a cardboard sign that Mama made for him, "help my family." There are glares of judgment and sympathy smirks from drivers as they pass us on the street in their nice warm cars. Those stares keep us frozen. Sometimes people hesitantly roll down their windows and reach out their hands, offering a morsel of sympathy, a gift of charity: a McDonald's card, a pair of gloves, a scarf or a snack bar. Never cash- cash could turn into drugs or whiskey- cause that's all homeless people want, I guess. They don't talk, just reach and retract their hand quickly so as to not touch our cold hands and "catch" the homelessness. Rapidly they roll up their window and look straight ahead, wishing so hard for the light to turn green so they can escape the awkwardness of the moment.

I hide behind Mama and Daddy on the sidewalk, what if my teacher was in the car, or worse, what if it was Sydney? I would die if someone from school saw me like this- cold, hungry, needy and without a place to go, no place to call home, except the red minivan. After a few hours of begging on the corner, Daddy had scored six bucks, a blanket, three pairs of gloves and a cup of coffee. It was enough to buy a small meal off the dollar menu of McDonalds and keep us warm for the week.

Chapter Fourteen: Winning and Losing

Daddy's not the only one who has been searching for a job, Mama has been trying to find work too. One day when we were walking around she found a sign asking for someone to help an elderly gentleman keep his house clean once a week. Mama used the prepaid phone that she and Daddy still had and called the number. After meeting with the man and his daughter just once, they hired Mama. It's just a few hours each week, but they said she could use the washer and dryer while she was there as long as she did his laundry too. It pays enough for us to have gas money for the van and Mama sometimes sneaks some bread or an apple from his kitchen without him noticing.

We don't really drive the van that much anymore, just enough to park it in different spots each night. We use it mostly to sleep in and sometimes Daddy will run the heat to help us warm up on really cold nights. Most nights we huddle together under our blankets to stay warm.

One day in March we parked the van a few blocks away from school and all went our separate ways for the day. Daddy walked from store to store, still looking for work, Mama went to clean the gentleman's house and Sarah, John and I went to school. When we met at the place where we left the van, we only saw each other- no van. "It must have been towed," Daddy informed us. The tags on the van had expired in June and I guess we left it in a no parking zone by accident. It didn't matter why they took it, but we knew we couldn't afford to go get it from the lot they towed it to. Our only possessions were gone- the storage unit had been cancelled a while ago due to non-payment and now the van with our duffle bags in it was gone too. The only things we owned were what we carried in our backpacks and what we wore on our bodies. There were no tears that day, I think we had just gotten so used to losing stuff, we just put our heads down and walked away, together.

I wish I could wish hard enough to escape the cold, escape the judgment and be "cured" from being homeless. No wish is strong enough to save us. I wish someone would reach out and help, ask me my name, treat me like a person, not just a body on the street.

Mama and Daddy seem to have lost their drive, their determination to find us an actual home. Daddy has stopped applying for jobs and Mama has become a master of food scavenging, finding clothing give aways and "safe" shelter for each night. She seems satisfied with the little bit she's earning from cleaning. I can't stand it. Sarah went to live with her boyfriend,

Sean, after we lost the van last week and after fighting with Mama. John let it slip at school that he had to sleep outside, so he is now staying with a foster family- I get to see him after school as he waits for his new mama to pick him up and I know he is safe and fed- and I am here with Mama and Daddy, just hoping tomorrow will be better.

Now I wonder. And wander. Wander and wonder. What happens next? I am out of everything including money, a change of clothes, friends and most of all, my hope is fading. Many community members have suggested we reach out to some of the local organizations to get help, but even trying to get to their office is a struggle. I am surrounded by unhappiness and loneliness even though my family is with me. I seem to cry for no reason and then I realize there is a reason. I have lost my way and no one is here to help me pick up the pieces. I long for the days of waking up to John shooting me in the face with Nerf Gun bullets and waiting impatiently for Sarah, the princess, to get out of the bathroom.

I still go to school each day that I can. Seeing the same kids each day gives me a sense of normalcy. I can hide behind my fake smile and pretend that I have a normal family, living in a normal house to go home to at the end of the day.

I miss my friends from St. Paul. I miss opening up my lunch box and finding a sandwich and an apple with a chocolate chip cookie. Most of all, I miss having a shoulder to lean on. No one in my family is strong enough to help fix the shattered mess.

Chapter Fifteen: The Library

After so much loss and loneliness, I am on a mission to find someone or something that would bring a bit of joy in to my world. Anything, a good meal, a full night's sleep or maybe even a ride on the swings at the park. I was too old for that but it didn't matter. If that made me giggle or shelter me from the outside for a few minutes, I would laugh off the teasing from the kids who thought I was too grown up for the swings. Never too old I thought. Playground equipment was there for everyone's pleasure and that would make me happy.

On my way to the park, I pass the library. Climbing the steps and passing through the large white columns, I could see a sign on the door that read "book sale." I know that I can't afford to buy any of the books, but it wouldn't hurt to go in and check out what they had. It would be something to do other than walk around and keep me from making a fool of myself on the swings at the park. I used to love to read. It is, or should it be "was" my passion, but with no school books and seeing only magazines that were months if not years old, I decided to check out the library and dream just a bit about what it would be like to buy a book that had just a $.50 price tag on it. The price didn't matter. Whatever the bargain sale price put on the book, well, I wouldn't have it anyway.

I tried to look presentable as I walked in the stoic building protected by four white columns outside of the main entrance. So far, no one gave me any mind so I kept trekking through the lobby, pretending that I belonged. I browsed the eight foot long tables like a real shopper would and even picked up a few books that were written for my age. The library lady came over and asked if I needed any help. I told her I was just looking and she graciously pointed to a couple of tables that might have selections with books of my liking.

She was nice to me and even asked my name and when I told her it was Tyler, she asked me to repeat it since my answer was muffled and barely audible. She said her name was Miss Gina and if I needed help with anything, she would be glad to point me in the right direction. Little did she know how much help I really needed.

I grabbed two books that had interesting covers and pictures of kids about my age on the inside pages. I picked a dark, out of the way corner to find a seat. It felt so good, the soft powder blue chair cushion and wooden arms of the chair as they wrapped around me. I had forgotten what anything that is comfortable felt like. I was quiet and unassuming and Miss Gina looked over and despite my grunginess, seemed to flash a smile at me now and then. Her deep blue eyes showed kindness and concern.

I think librarians are smarter than we even think because something told me she knew more than she led on. I prayed she couldn't detect the stench under my coat or see the grime that had built up in my fingernails. That wasn't who I was or what I was about but that had become the new me.

Sitting in the library was more than just reading a book or two. It was about trying to get my teenaged dignity back and someone being nice to me without staring me down. It was just the lift I needed. The library stayed open till 8 pm and I wanted to milk every last minute out of the grandfather clock that chimed every fifteen minutes in the corner by the copy machine. Miss Gina even offered me a piece of hard candy. The kind that old people carry in their pockets. But Miss Gina wasn't that old and the candy, some flavor I never even tasted, seemed like a real treat for me. Maybe it was butterscotch or maybe that odd fruit in the grocery store that no one buys...I think it's called a mango. Some sort of jungle flavored fruit.

Deciding it was time to retreat and find what's left of my family, I put the books back and thanked Miss Gina for the help. She suggested I come back tomorrow and there would be even more books. I thanked her for the invitation and replied that I would try to come back. After all, what else did I have to do?

Leaving the library I began to feel a sliver of hope. Someone wants to see me tomorrow, even if it is only some lady at the library, and Miss Gina probably told everyone to come back, someone just might care. Walking down the street with the library behind me, I glance over at Mc Donald's and see Mama there near the dumpster, waiting for a chance that she can sneak to get tonight's dinner. The street lights cast a dim shadow, her face looks hallow. Every bit of food she gets, she gives to Daddy and me, only eating after we are done, and even then if she sees another family with hungry eyes she will give them her last morsel. Sarah and John leaving us broke her. She works so hard to take care of us and keep our family together, but it just got too hard for John to hide his homelessness from his teacher and Sarah couldn't handle being cold, un-showered and hungry anymore.

Ahead of me, on the dark Memphis street, stood Daddy. His backpack laden with blankets and a few spare clothing items he had found for us. I joined Daddy and we waited silently for Mama to return with dinner. The hunger in the pit of my stomach was an open hole, I knew whatever spare French fries or half eaten cheeseburger was not going to satisfy it, but I was grateful and would tell Mama that I was full just so she would eat a little too.

As we walked and ate, I told Mama and Daddy about Miss Gina and the library book sale and how she invited me back tomorrow. Mama said I can go back, but not to let Miss Gina ask any questions, John's teacher asked too many questions and got him taken away. Sometimes I just want to be taken away- away to somewhere warm with food- but no one asks me about my family, my home, and my dirty clothes or worn out shoes. I guess no one cares enough to ask or they are too afraid of the answers, just like Mama is terrified of the questions.

Mama, Daddy, and I walk until we find a vacant stair well next to a dark building, somewhere safe and out of the spring wind to rest for the night. Daddy spreads out a blanket for us to sit on and covers us with the other blanket from his backpack. He offers his backpack to Mama as a pillow and puts his arm around her. I turn with my back to them and try to drift off into sleep. When we first started to sleep on the streets, it was hard to shiver myself to sleep, but now my body is getting used to being cold and I'm too exhausted to fight sleep. I close my eyes and steal a few moments of paradise in my dreams only to be awoken by a bright light shining in my tired eyes. We've been found again. A security guard beams his frightening flash light in our sleeping faces- I wish I could say that this frightened me, but it's happened so many times- I know the drill. Be respectful, say yes sir, I'm sorry sir, pack up quickly, put your head down and walk away together. The security guards don't want any trouble and neither do we. They won't turn us into the cops if we cooperate, so we do. The guy in the stair well, a few feet away, doesn't know the rules or he just doesn't care and he is yelling and cussing. We walk fast, because we know the cops will be comin' and we don't want no part of that. Sometimes, people put up a fight just so the cops will take them to jail- that way they get a place to sleep and shower and a few meals before they are let out on the streets again.

    Walking the dark Memphis streets in the middle of the night has become a habit for us. We walk until we find an open gas station, somewhere we can use the facilities, get a drink of water from the sink and warm up for a quick minute before we get kicked out of there too. There's a new attendant behind the register, they don't know that last night's worker shooed us out and told us to never come back. They don't know that this gas station is the closest thing we have to a home or that we don't have enough money to even purchase a stick of gum. Mama used her cleaning money this week to buy a little bit of food, some peanut butter, apples and crackers- which we devoured in a couple of days. We move quickly so not to bother them and exit the station without making eye contact.

As we look for a new resting spot, we play a strange game of hide and seek- where the objective is to not find someone. Of course, on a cool March morning, about 2 a.m., all of the good spots are full- bodies slumped over each other, using body heat to keep warm. Finally, around 4 a.m. we stumble upon a vacant building with an open door- others have found it before us, but there's enough room in the hallway for us to huddle and get an hour or so of sleep before we get up, so I can go to school and Mama and Daddy can do nothing.

Throughout the school day, all I can think about is Miss Gina, the book sale and the comfortable blue chair. I tell Sydney about the book sale and invite her to come with me to the library, but she has to babysit her siblings after school, so she can't join me this time.

As soon as the school bell rings, I race out the door and down the street to the library, hoping to find another treasure to read, hoping my soft blue chair is available, hoping to be greeted by Miss Gina's smiling face and hoping to keep my homelessness a secret.

"Hi Tyler, I am so glad you came back!" Miss Gina beams as she opens the library's glass door for me and a few other teenage patrons.

Miss Gina greets the others, asking how they are, what they've been doing, etc. The exact polite inquiries that I am desperate to avoid. I offer an obligatory smile, then force my eyes down to the floor and head for "my" blue chair to check if it is occupied.

After seeing that my chair is waiting for me, unoccupied, I begin to wander through the young adult section of the library. Mama used to take Sarah, John and I to the library for Saturday story time when we were younger. I have fond memories of going to the

Cordova Public Library to experience puppet shows, Dr. Seuss books, and the like. In the summers we would join the summer reading club. Mama would sign us up and encourage (force) us to read each week to earn a prize- a gift certificate for bowling or pizza. I would embrace the challenge of reading as many books as I possibly could in a summer and earning every single prize available! Sarah, on the other hand, would only read what Mama forced her to, so she could win a prize each week. Then there was John- Mama even read his books to him, but he couldn't sit still long enough to finish very many. Inevitably John wouldn't earn his prizes, so Mama would have to pay for him to have pizza and go bowling. I thought she should make him watch us have fun without him, but apparently Mama thought that was cruel.

Do they still have summer reading programs? Would they let a teenager, like me, participate? I could go for free pizza or a game of bowling- anything to make me feel normal, look normal. Who am I kidding? Normal was six months ago.

"Tyler? Hey, I found some books from the books sale that I thought you might enjoy." Miss Gina appeared with an offering of books by James Patterson- one of my favorite authors.

"How did you know I like James Patterson books?"

"Just a guess. He's a great author and lots of kids your age gravitate towards books like his. Here, when you're done reading these, return them to me and I'll help you pick out a few more."

Miss Gina walked away, towards the library's help desk and left me with the treasures she had bestowed upon me- books. Books that can take me away to an alternate universe. *Witch & Wizard* captures my attention first, "For 15-year-old Wisty and her older brother Whit, life turns upside down when they are torn from their parents one night and slammed into a secret prison for no reason they can comprehend. The New Order, as it is known, is clearly trying to suppress Life, Liberty, and the Pursuit of Being a Normal Teenager." I could write my own book about being suppressed from being a normal teenager, having your life turned upside down and being held captive in a prison without a home.

Seated comfortably in the corner in the inviting blue chair, I peruse Patterson's pages. Around page 50, a brochure falls in my lap, "Teen Summer Reading Volunteers." There's a handwritten note on the front- "Tyler, I hope you'll join us this summer. – Miss Gina."

After a few hours of reading, the lights begin to dim, it must be time to go …… home. I wonder where home will be tonight. Leaving the library, I notice a dark stair well, warm and vacant; it's not until I get closer that I notice it isn't vacant, it's occupied by someone else. Choosing a corner to hide in, I slump in the shadows of the hallway- trying to make myself disappear. Listening closely to the sound of footsteps as they get quieter, I hear the final door close and wait-listening for silence. My eyes close, in the comfort of my own shadow, I drift to sleep.

"Pssst, boy, do you want some?" A fellow teen boy, one that walked into the library with me yesterday, wakens me- offering a bag of chips. "Miss Gina left a bag of snacks on the stairs, you want some?"

"What? Why would she leave chips on the stairs? Who are you?" I stutter, trying to make sense of the boy in front of me.

"Chips. Do you want some chips? I'm William. What are you doing here?" I hesitantly pick out a hand full of the salty round snack and place them one at a time in my mouth, enjoying every crunch.

William walks away, leaving me to ponder the questions that are arising in my head. I can hear William whispering a few more times, there must be more people in this seemingly vacant hallway. Does Miss Gina leave food every night? Does she know people stay here? How many people are here? Are they like me? Does Mama miss me? Did Daddy notice? This isn't the first night we've been apart, sometimes it's hard to find each other when you don't have a home at which to meet. Sleep comes to me again- it's nice to not be cold. In the morning, William nudges me awake- "The library is open, Miss Gina isn't here yet, so be careful no one sees you coming out of the hallway," he disappears.

Chapter Sixteen: Finding Hope

Mama meets me across the street from school in the morning. I tell her about my second trip to the library, William, chips, and the James Patterson books. She nods and listens, I don't think she slept last night. She agrees to meet me here after school and go to the library with me- I'm afraid for Miss Gina to meet her, but excited at the same time. For once, I'm not afraid if Miss Gina finds out that I'm homeless- I'm just hopeful that maybe Mama could get some rest. Daddy could use the computer at the library to look for a job and maybe, just maybe, we could get help. I overheard Miss Gina tell someone else about a job fair, maybe she could tell Daddy about it too. I quickly kiss Mama on the cheek and head into school.

School takes forever- teachers talking and talking and talking. The same thing happens in every class- the teacher talks, the students take notes, homework is assigned, notes are written and passed, some assignments get done and then the bell rings. I'm usually a fairly good student, if I'm not too tired or hungry, but today I can only think of returning to the library.

After school, I rush out the door to meet Mama and see that she brought Daddy too. As John exits school, walking with his friends, he waves at the three of us. His foster mama won't allow him to cross the street and talk to us, but seeing him clean, fed and rested, even if from a distance, reassures us that he is in a good place.

Mama, Daddy and I walk together to the library. Mama asks about my day and nods along as I tell her about my classes and Sydney. I tell Daddy about Miss Gina and the job fair she was talking about. Daddy agrees to find out what he can. Upon entering the library, Miss Gina isn't at the door today, but there's a new stack of books on my blue chair. I settle down in the old blue chair to begin perusing the selection she left for me, Mama wanders through the non-fiction, self-help books- looking for her favorite Christian authors, while Daddy sits in front of a computer to look for a job. Miss Gina casually drops some resume workshop, and job finder brochures next to Daddy's elbow. I don't know how she does it, it's like she can read minds. She must sense our needs.

A year ago, I wished John would be less annoying, Sarah would stop being so prissy, and that Daddy and Mama would buy us more presents. This year, I just wish we could be together. Miss Gina may be our angel of hope. I glance up from my book to see her talking with Mama- I wish I could hear what they're saying, Mama's smiling and nodding. For a minute, I imagine that we have a home to go to at the end of the day. For a minute, I think that Sarah and John will join us at the library and we will all be together.

Mama comes over to me and pulls up a nice wooden chair. She tells me that Miss Gina suggested we stay until the library closes and that the library is looking to hire someone to sort books as they are returned. Mama is going to have Miss Gina help her apply for the job in the morning.

As the lights begin to flicker around 8 o'clock, the library's closing time, we wait casually for most of the patrons to exit. Right before we would exit the library, I motion for Mama and Daddy to go down the dark stairway. We find a recessed doorway downstairs to relax in until the librarians' footsteps disappear. Once the silence has filled the building William brings around a basket of fruit that

Miss Gina happened to leave on the stairs along with a pamphlet for inexpensive housing for those in need.

Eating our fruit and huddling together, we smile. The future is still unknown, but right now, today, there is hope.

Made in the USA
San Bernardino, CA
14 September 2015